"For the weary, the discouraged, the sick, and the suffering, the psalms of lament express the anguish of our souls. In *Crying Out to God: Experiencing Grace through Psalms of Lament*, Wendy Alsup offers a faithful and tender guide through these songs of sorrow. With wisdom and compassion, she helps readers bring their pain before the Lord while holding fast to his comfort and grace. This study is a balm for those walking through suffering—and for those who walk beside them."

Melissa Kruger, author and vice president of discipleship at The Gospel Coalition

"Many of us long to pour out our unfiltered protests to God but wonder if it's allowed. Through the psalms of lament, *Crying Out to God* shows that our cries are not only permitted but invited. With vulnerable storytelling, biblical insight, and thoughtful questions, Wendy Alsup leads readers into the richness and power of lament. This study doesn't just teach—it helps you practice lament as a way to draw near to God. I wholeheartedly recommend this book."

Vaneetha Rendall Risner, author of *Watching for the Morning* and *Walking Through Fire*

WENDY ALSUP

CRYING OUT TO GOD

Experiencing Grace Through Psalms of Lament

An imprint of InterVarsity Press
Downers Grove, Illinois

InterVarsity Press
P.O. Box 1400 | Downers Grove, IL 60515-1426
ivpress.com | email@ivpress.com

InterVarsity Press® is the publishing division of InterVarsity Christian Fellowship/USA®. For more information, visit intervarsity.org.

While any stories in this book are true, some names and identifying information may have been changed to protect the privacy of individuals.

The publisher cannot verify the accuracy or functionality of website URLs used in this book beyond the date of publication.

Cover design: Faceout Studio, Tim Green
Interior design: Daniel van Loon
Cover images: © Malte Mueller / fStop via Getty Images; © saemilee / DigitalVision Vectors via Getty Images

ISBN 978-1-5140-1089-1 (print) | ISBN 978-1-5140-1090-7 (digital)

Printed in the United States of America ♾

Library of Congress Cataloging-in-Publication Data
Names: Alsup, Wendy Horger, 1970- author
Title: Crying out to God : experiencing grace through Psalms of lament : an 8-week bible study with video access / Wendy Alsup.
Description: Downers Grove, IL : IVP, [2026] | Series: IVP Bible study experience
Identifiers: LCCN 2025020381 (print) | LCCN 2025020382 (ebook) | ISBN 9781514010891 paperback | ISBN 9781514010907 ebook
Subjects: LCSH: Bible. Lamentations–Criticism, interpretation, etc. | Bible–Study and teaching | Laments in the Bible
Classification: LCC BS1535.52 .A47 2026 (print) | LCC BS1535.52 (ebook) | DDC 224/.3–dc23/eng/20250923
LC record available at https://lccn.loc.gov/2025020381
LC ebook record available at https://lccn.loc.gov/2025020382

33 32 31 30 29 28 27 26 | 13 12 11 10 9 8 7 6 5 4 3 2 1

CONTENTS

INTRODUCTION

Blessed are those who mourn, for they will be comforted.

Matthew 5:4

All is not right in our world today. Sometimes the pain and suffering in the world is right at our doorstep, in our faces, oozing through our homes and bodies. Other times, even when not facing obvious sources of suffering, many of us feel a low-level current of discouragement running in the background of our lives. Disappointment, demoralization, and cynicism infiltrate our days. If they haven't yet, they will.

However it manifests, *we all have something to mourn*. We are all daily affected by something that is wrong in the world, something that is not consistent with God's perfect creation in the Garden of Eden.

Where do you find yourself today? Are you mourning profound loss personally? Maybe you are walking with someone who is navigating deep grief. Perhaps, like myself and other close friends, you have experienced the loss of a loved one through death, and this loss is a haze that hovers over each moment of your day. Maybe your loved one still lives but has rejected God and you. Are you haunted by this person's memory instead of comforted by it?

Maybe you, like me, are facing debilitating illness. Do you labor to complete the bare minimum of tasks you need to do each day? Have you received a diagnosis that you grapple to make sense of? Do you have a child or loved one who is struggling emotionally, spiritually, or physically? We often carry the burdens and pain of those we love as if they are our own.

The list could go on and on. Perhaps your suffering, on a spectrum, does not seem as dark as others'. Even so, job stresses, financial issues, church strain, and family struggles can push us into a dark place where we wrestle with God and others. You don't have to compare your suffering to others to find help in this study; you don't even have to be aware of suffering in your

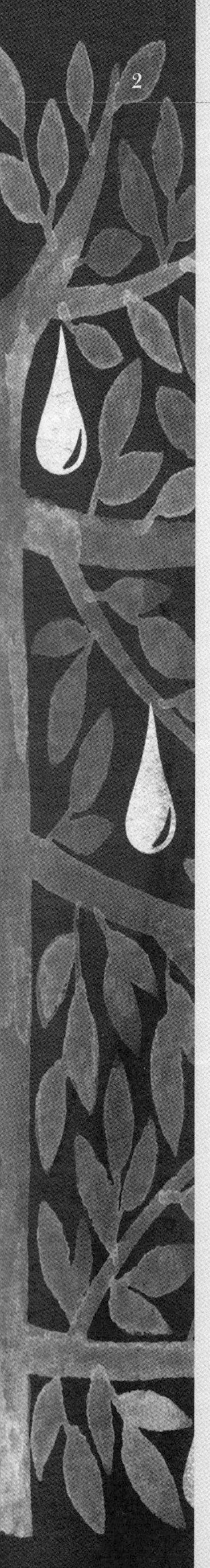

own life. Our stories and experiences of suffering are wide and varied. But grief and mourning are universal.

The disillusionment believers face around suffering leads to a host of questions: Why does God allow suffering into our lives and the lives of those we love? Why does suffering seem to come upon so many who do not deserve it, while those who perpetuate injustice seem to avoid consequences for the pain they have caused? Such questions over suffering, injustice, and the general unfairness of the world are oft-cited reasons for doubt, or even leaving the faith. How do we respond when these questions arise in us and in those we love? How do we maintain hope for others when they struggle to hope for themselves?

How do we maintain hope for *ourselves*?

Jesus said, "Blessed are those who mourn, for they will be comforted" (Matthew 5:4). Does Jesus' assurance ring hollow to you? Suffering doesn't feel like a blessing. In fact, it may feel as though it alienates you or your loved one from God. Such was the feeling of many writers God used to pen the chapters of the Bible we will be studying for the next eight weeks.

If God is good, why is my life bad? If God is light, why does my body seem consumed by darkness? If God is just, why am I experiencing long-term injustice? If God is love, why am I experiencing hate and betrayal? If God is life, why am I dying? If you haven't personally wrestled with these questions, I guarantee you know someone who has. The writers of Scripture certainly wrestled with such questions.

The bottom line is that suffering can tempt believers to doubt what they know of God, his people, and his Word. If God, the church, and the Scriptures are good, why aren't they good for me or my loved ones? We need something outside ourselves to ground us in Someone bigger than ourselves. We need to anchor to a rock that is heavier than our frame, that can hold us tight as we feel tossed about. Over the next eight weeks, we will use lament in Scripture to name the very real emotions we face as we suffer and to understand the character of our God who anchors us amid the emotional and physical storms suffering causes.

The word *lament* in the Bible simply means weeping or mourning. But the category of lament in the Scriptures is bigger than the mere word suggests. Lament in the Psalms is more than grief or mourning, it is grief expressed *to God*. It is mourning in relationship with the God of the universe, and we find in the Scriptures that Christ shares this grief with us. We do not lament alone. God's Word, through its example of lament, helps us name our suffering and face it head-on.

Psalms of lament generally begin with an acknowledgment of God, move quickly into raw complaint, and end with hope in the unchanging character and glory of God that secures us in the storm. The foundational thought that will anchor us each week of this study is that the act of lament—that is, the expression and experience of bringing our complaints to God as he models for us in the Scriptures—is a means of God's grace. It is a channel through which God gifts us the help to persevere and the hope for our times of struggle.

Some of us may not particularly want to open the heavy gate that guards us from dark emotions over suffering in our world. Be encouraged as we explore the deep emotions and questions suffering provokes: The Holy Spirit groans with us when we have no words, bringing our needs before the Father in prayer (Romans 8:26). God pays "attention to the prayer of the destitute and will not despise their prayer" (Psalm 102:17). God keeps track of our sorrows and collects our tears (Psalm 56:8). The last scene of Scripture in Revelation has God wiping the tears gently from our faces with his own hand. Though ignoring the dark thoughts suffering provokes may provide temporary peace, there is a deeper, better peace to be had when we face suffering head-on and bring our dark emotions and questions directly to God.

For the next eight weeks, join me in exploring the dark, the hard, the *wrong* with this world. Name it before the Lord and allow God through the Scriptures to meet you in it, that you may find grace in your time of need, your community's time of need, and our world's time of need. God has not left us to journey through our dark emotions alone.

I cry aloud to God,
aloud to God, and he will hear me.

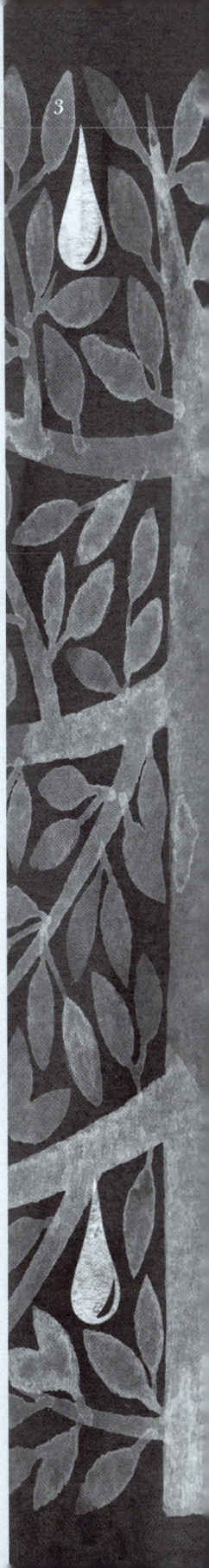

PSALM 77:1

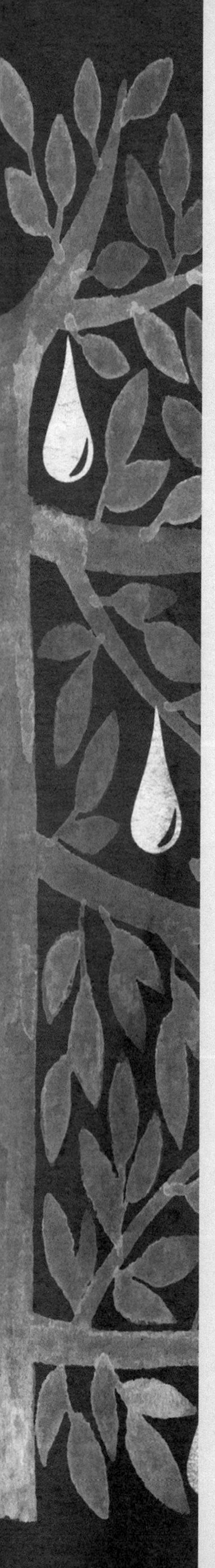

HOW TO USE THIS BOOK

Whether you are engaging in this study with a large group, a small group, in a coffee shop with a friend, or by yourself in your favorite chair, here are some helpful suggestions.

FOR THE GROUP SESSION

Set aside a designated day and time for a weekly gathering—in person or virtually—for the next eight weeks. The content (video and discussion) will take about an hour, but I recommend allowing some additional time for a check-in or to share prayer requests.

The videos are accessed through the QR code in the book. These videos were created with a group in mind—that you would watch the video together and then immediately engage in the content that follows. But it also means that individuals still have access, which is nice if someone has to miss a group gathering.

A few tips on engaging in a group discussion:

- Be willing to participate in the discussion. The leader of your group will moderate the conversation, and it helps them to have willing participants.
- Be careful not to dominate the discussion. We are sometimes so eager to express our thoughts that we leave too little opportunity for others to respond. By all means participate, but also make space for the insight of others.
- Be sensitive to other members of the group. Listen attentively and ask follow up questions when appropriate. You might be surprised by others' insights!
- Stick to the topic being discussed and try to avoid "rabbit trails."
- Remember that anything said in the group is considered confidential and should not be discussed outside the group unless specific permission is given to do so.

If you have time, a good check-in question might be to name a highlight from the previous week of study—either from the group session or individual days. This study was designed so that you can still participate in the Group Session even if you haven't done all the homework, but—of course—I hope you'll still want to engage with everything!

FOR THE INDIVIDUAL DAYS

Following the Group Session are five days of content for you to engage with during the week between group gatherings. I believe you will find the content meaningful but not overwhelming, and it's designed to fit into your normal, everyday life.

A few tips for engaging in individual study and reflection:

- Have a designated Bible you use for this study that you are willing to mark up. If you don't have one, you can always print off and mark up each week's psalm individually. Most of the Scripture I reference is taken from the Christian Standard Bible (CSB).
- As you begin each day, there are prompts to invite God to speak to you through his Word. Prayer and Bible reading are the most important part of each day's study. Don't rush past them.
- Write your answers to the questions in the spaces provided or in a journal. Writing can bring clarity and deeper understanding.
- At the end of each day, thank God for what you have learned and pray about any applications that have come to mind.

Though written thousands of years ago, Scripture is living and active (Hebrews 4:12), and God still speaks through it today. May God speak to you through his Word in this study in ways that are ***helpful*** and ***hopeful*** as you navigate suffering in your life and community.

WEEK ONE | HELP, LORD—PSALM 12

Group Session Introduction

For the next eight weeks, we will look at how Scripture helps us articulate our grief, encompassing everything from sadness or distress to anguished suffering. We will learn to speak that grief—and groan when we do not have words—to the One who carries the weight of suffering with and for us. We will discover the supernatural help he gives us as we cry out to him over the wounds we bear.

Hebrews 4:16 is a key passage with our overarching theme for the next eight weeks:

> *Therefore, let us approach the throne of grace with boldness, so that we may receive mercy and find grace to help us in time of need.*

Watch this week's video.

DISCUSSION

Before we begin our study of psalms of lament, it may be helpful to recognize our own experience of suffering and the tension we have felt with God and other Christians because of it. With respect for the varying degrees with which each group member feels free to share, discuss these questions and learn more about one another.

- We have defined *suffering* as "our groaning under the weight of humanity's fall." Keeping this definition in mind, what kinds of suffering have you seen in your community? In our nation? In the world?
- What hurtful responses have you witnessed to suffering in your community?
- What helpful, compassionate responses to suffering have you seen or experienced?

- How have you observed others dealing with their own suffering, in both helpful and harmful ways?
- Consider not why you are suffering, but what suffering looks like in your life. How can suffering affect us mentally, emotionally, and relationally?
- How can suffering cause us to question the church, the Scriptures, or God himself?
- Read Hebrews 4:16. What does its truth teach us about the purpose of lament?
- Read Hebrews 2:10. This passage refers to Jesus as the pioneer in our suffering. Like a Coast Guard ice cutter ship, Jesus plowed ahead of us through unknown territory, clearing the way for those who followed. Sometimes we feel like pioneers in our suffering, alone as we trailblaze through unfamiliar paths. How can thinking of Jesus as the pioneer and trailblazer ahead of us be an encouragement in suffering?

This week, as we consider Psalm 12, we will find that creation, God the Spirit, and God the Son all groan *with us* under the weight of all that is wrong in the world after the fall. Be encouraged that God has not left us alone to carry these weights by ourselves.

In the closing prayer, bring the following to God:

- The spiritual tension raised by the types of suffering mentioned in the discussion.
- Thanks that Jesus has gone through suffering ahead of us.
- Praise for the grace and mercy God promises us in these hard days.

I AM INTRIGUED by the word *groan*. It points to a response to our trials that precedes and transcends words. I need and want to cry out to God, but I can't articulate a word. I have groaned: in the waiting area of a psychiatric ward. In the ICU after cancer surgery. On the floor of my living room after signing divorce papers. In my car in the wake of a church conflict I didn't see coming. I groaned and cried out to God with grief and fear I couldn't put into words.

We are all affected by suffering—in our homes, our communities, and our world. And our hearts cry out because we know this is not how things are supposed to be! In the opening video, I defined *suffering* as our groaning under the weight of humanity's fall. We can read in Genesis 3 how God created a perfect world and placed Adam and Eve in the middle of it with the words "It was good." But Satan tempted Adam and Eve to disbelieve and disobey God. They did, and as a result everything broke. Sin, sickness, broken relationships, and death entered the world, and humanity has groaned under this weight ever since.

The problems that came into the world after the fall are deep and pervasive. They extend through our bodies, hearts, and the world around us. The weight of humanity's fall on our lives is real. There is no value in pretending it doesn't exist, and the Bible doesn't demand we make peace with it. Instead, Scripture tells us that as we groan, all of creation groans with us.

> For we know that the whole creation has been groaning together with labor pains until now. Not only that, but we ourselves who have the Spirit as the firstfruits—we also groan within ourselves, eagerly waiting for adoption, the redemption of our bodies. (Romans 8:22-23)

Today, as we begin our look at lament in Scripture, we will find help to name the things about which we groan and to bring them to God in prayer.

First, what is lament?

The simplest definition of *lament* is "weeping" or "mourning." We associate words like *weeping* and *mourning* with grief, a significant aspect of lament. It is more than grief, though; it is grief expressed—technically, a complaint. But it's also more than a complaint. What makes lament so unique is that it is grief and complaint expressed to God. It is weeping and mourning in relationship *with God*. Remarkably, God does not abandon us in our pain. And in fact, he welcomes our lament and shares in our suffering.

Most psalms of lament follow a pattern of turning to God in despair, pouring out a complaint, and concluding with a declaration of trust in God. This week, Psalm 12 will guide our lament. It will give us language to name what is wrong with the world, and why it makes sense that we groan.

You will read through the psalm slowly three times. Pray before and between each reading: *Lord, open my eyes to your supernatural help through this psalm. Help me to name the emotional, spiritual, and physical struggles I face in this pervasively broken world.*

On your first two readings, try to take in the entire psalm. Then on the third reading, note words or phrases that stand out to you. You might notice words that reveal the world's brokenness. You might notice words that describe God's character and response. Or maybe you notice something else. Circle any phrases that stand out to you. (If you'd prefer, there is also space below to list those words and phrases.)

Read Psalm 12.

- Look back through the words and phrases you identified. Which phrases describe results of the fall that you are experiencing personally right now? How have you experienced unfaithfulness, disloyalty, or lies against you or God?

- In verse 5, the psalmist says that God sees the devastation of the needy, and he responds to the groans of the poor. If you have felt something too deep for words under the weight that you carry, describe that feeling.

- I'm convinced that the more suffering we experience in life, the fewer words we possess to articulate it. After all, what words are there that could possibly ease our pain? And so we groan.

> "Because of the devastation of the needy
> and the groaning of the poor,
> I will now rise up," says the LORD.
> "I will provide safety for the one who longs for it." (Psalm 12:5)

This verse is a sweet help to us as we groan under our own weight of suffering. Notice how God *doesn't* respond—he doesn't rebuke the groaning of the needy. He does not tell them to have more faith, nor does he characterize their groans as sinful complaints. Instead, God says he will arise and provide safety in response to their groans.

Today, in closing, I invite you to face head-on the emotional, physical, and spiritual weights you carry because of the world's brokenness. In the space below or in a journal, write out whatever words you have now for God, and groan without words what you cannot yet articulate. Through this study, Scripture will help you name your struggles more specifically.

For he has not despised
or abhorred
the torment of the oppressed.
He did not hide his
face from him
but listened when he
cried to him for help.

PSALM 22:24

TODAY, WE WILL READ Psalm 12:1-5 again. But today's focus is on the first element of biblical lament: the initial turning to God. Remember, lament has an honest quality to it.

PSALM 12:1-5

DAY 2

The mourning and crying sound like complaints because they are. When the complaint is directed to God, the Creator of the universe who holds all of time in his hands, then it becomes lament.

Our usual practice will be to pray, asking God to open our eyes to his help to us in Scripture, and then to read our passage three times slowly. Pray between each reading: *Father in heaven, open my eyes to your help for me through this psalm of lament. On the third reading, note words or phrases that stand out to you.*

Read Psalm 12:1-5.

- As you read today, what words or phrases stood out to you? Was there anything new that you didn't note yesterday?

Notice David's opening words, "Help, Lord." Because it's such a simple phrase, it's easy to gloss over it. *Yet directing our complaint directly to God is the most essential element of biblical lament.* Have you struggled in your life with turning to God with your complaints?

My husband experienced the onset of symptoms of schizophrenia in 2012 and divorced me in 2015. My children were nine and eleven years old at the time. In those two sentences lie years of painful, confusing days trying to understand and navigate the circumstances devastating my family. I had dear friends in town and out of town whom I called regularly when I needed to process what was happening, usually at least once a day. But I noticed over time that it was only when none of my friends were available that I would finally be forced to turn to God.

- Who are your go-to friends or family when you need to talk through grief or stress with someone?

- Why can it be hard to turn to God when we are suffering? What mental hurdles stand in your way when you feel overwhelmed with pain?

David's initial cry to God was simply, "Help." The Hebrew word for help that David uses is most often translated "deliver" or "save." This cry is one of desperation. It is the drowning man reaching his hand toward the approaching lifeguard. It is the climber clinging to the side of a mountain on a tiny overhang, calling to the search and rescue team above her. It is the child running from an attacking dog toward their father who will gather them up and keep them safe. It reveals desperation on the part of the one crying out. But the object of our cry is the One who is able to help, deliver, and save.

- What circumstances in your life or the lives of your loved ones have caused you to feel desperation?

After David cries to God, he lays out his complaint, which we will explore tomorrow. But for now, take a closer look at how God responds in verse 5.

"Because of the devastation of the needy
and the groaning of the poor,
I will now rise up," says the Lord.
"I will provide safety for the one who longs for it."

- What stands out to you about God's response to David's cry?

I am struck that it was not David's poetic words that caused God to rise up; it was the devastation of the needy and the groaning of the poor. The devastated don't need fancy prayers—which is good, because at my worst points it has been beyond me to articulate anything coherent to God. And as we saw in day one, God doesn't rebuke our groanings. But even when we have no words, God receives and acts upon our simple cries.

As we close today, I will give you words to pray, but you can know you do not need words to bring your pain to God. Pray with words or simply groan. Either way, he hears and responds to our prayers directed to him.

Lord, I need your help today. My family needs your help. My community needs your help. My church needs your help. Sin and suffering have devastated so much. Deliver me, my family, and my church. Help us to persevere and hope. Thank you that you hear my groaning even when I cannot articulate all that I need.

PSALM 12:1-5

DAY 3

We have read through all or part of Psalm 12 around six times, but there is more in David's cry to God. We are going to read part of it again. Pray between each reading: *Father, help me through your Scriptures today. Open my eyes to aid I have not yet seen in my previous readings*. On your third reading, note anything new that stands out to you that you had not focused on before.

READ PSALM 12:1-5.

- What stood out to you today in this reading?

I am struck by the psalmist's language of betrayal. Loyalty had disappeared from the earth. In David's view of the moment, no one remained faithful. Everyone said what they thought David wanted to hear to his face, while conspiring his demise behind his back. Psalm 12 is often related chronologically to the events of 2 Samuel 15–16. That passage tells the story of King David's son Absalom who revolted against him. David was betrayed by his own son and by close advisors who sided with his son against him. This was devastating to David and many around him.

> David was climbing the slope of the Mount of Olives, weeping as he ascended. His head was covered, and he was walking barefoot. All the people with him covered their heads and went up, weeping as they ascended. (2 Samuel 15:30)

- How have you, your loved one, or your community experienced disloyalty, betrayal, or unfaithfulness? What was the fallout in your life or in the community's life?

Disloyalty. Betrayal by family and close friends. Unfaithfulness to a committed relationship. All are ultimately results of Adam and Eve's first sin. Back in the Garden of Eden, Adam turned on his wife, flesh of his flesh. He threw her under the bus the moment God questioned him about his sin (Genesis 3:12). Betrayal and disloyalty have marred personal relationships ever since, and they still devastate us when they show up in our lives.

And we groan.

David groaned particularly over the betrayal he faced by trusted friends and family. Betrayals in our biological or spiritual families are particularly devastating.

- Why is unfaithfulness in a trusted relationship so devastating emotionally and/or spiritually?

I will never forget the day my husband brought home divorce papers from a lawyer and handed them to me to fill out (I didn't). We had made vows to one another in front of God and family that, in my head at least, bound us together for life. We had forged our life together through many hard seasons financially, physically, and spiritually. Each season seemed to bring us together more strongly.

He was my safe person. Though he had been resistant to taking medications for the symptoms of schizophrenia he experienced, on the day he handed me the divorce papers, he seemed fully in control of himself. That moment broke something in me I'm not sure I'll ever fully recover from in this life.

In Psalm 12, God offers us solidarity for such moments and invites us to pour out our devastation to him for help and deliverance. The psalmist reminds us that God will provide safety—in all the places and circumstances that have made us feel unsafe. As we close today, I invite you to bring directly to God the situations of betrayal, disloyalty, and unfaithfulness you have faced. Name the harm done to you or your loved ones. Ask God for help, salvation, deliverance, and safety. Write out your prayer below.

PSALM 12:5-8 — **DAY 4**

TODAY, WE WILL READ Psalm 12:5-8. Remember the form that laments tend to take: an initial calling out to God, then complaint to God over the brokenness of the world, followed by affirmations of God's character and trust in him. For many of us, it will take longer than a few verses to move from complaint to trust, and we will look at psalms in this study that do not resolve so easily. Psalm 12 holds this classic pattern, but it too ends with a somber reflection of things that remain wrong in this world. It is okay if you are not yet at the place of trusting God as David did in these verses, but perhaps reading his words will help you know what is possible through the gift of lament.

Using the same practice as before, first pray and ask God for help to trust him through this psalm. Then read it three times slowly, noting words or phrases that stand out to you on your final reading.

READ PSALM 12:5-8.

- What words or phrases stood out to you in today's reading? How do those phrases reflect on situations in your own life right now?

- Did anything new stand out to you about God's response to the groaning of the needy?

- What does David affirm about God's character in verse 6?

Yesterday, we considered the experience of betrayal. David was deeply hurt by people who flattered him to his face while plotting to overthrow him behind his back. The contrast in verse 6 is clear. *Others may flatter or betray, but God's words are pure.* In fact, they are the purest of pure, refined over and over again until what is left is all that is true, good, and trustworthy.

- How do you understand the language of verse 6? Rephrase it in your own words.

God's words are pure, and they are helpful. You can count on, hold on to, and trust the words God says in Scripture. This affirmation is meaningful to me. I was deeply broken by my spouse's betrayal of our vows, breaking his word to me. I have come to be very sensitive about this in my family, sitting down my boys and ex-husband (who remains in our lives as my children's father) recently to ask simply, "Please don't tell me you are going to do something you aren't going to do. Just tell me you don't want to do it." Every new time someone tells me something to my face without planning to follow through exposes old wounds in my heart. When David cries out against betrayal, lying, and unfaithfulness, I feel it deeply. As a result, when David affirms the ultimate purity and faithfulness of God's words, it is a balm to my parched soul.

Others may speak flippantly with no thought of following through. But God's words are tested and pure. Lying is antithetical to his character. When God says he will rise up and provide safety for the one who longs for it, he will surely do it.

- How have others hurt you by being unfaithful to their word?

- How does God's faithfulness help you navigate betrayal?

As we close, pray through the passage we read, personalizing it as a response to God.

God, you see our devastation and hear our groaning. You promise to rise up and provide safety to us who long for it. I long for it, God! The psalmist says your words are the purest of pure. Others have lied and not kept their promises. But your promises are tried and true. I am wounded by the ways others have broken their word to me. Help me believe that I can count on your words.

DAY 5

ROMANS 8:26 AND HEBREWS 4:15-16

In this study, we are guided by several principles that have already been at play in Psalm 12. First, we are not alone in our suffering. The psalms of lament are just one of many places in Scripture we find solidarity when we are experiencing suffering that feels deeply alienating. Further in our study, Job, Joseph, Hagar, and other psalmists like Asaph also offer us companionship in our suffering.

But it isn't just other humans who suffer with us: Christ himself suffers with us. And in Romans 8:26, we see that God the Holy Spirit groans with us when we have no words. It is an amazing comfort to know that we are not left to navigate our suffering by ourselves and that Christ himself suffers with us.

A second principle is this: lament is a means of God's grace to us in our need. Hebrews 4:16, a passage we will return to again and again, says that *prayer is a conduit of God's grace*, and lament is the most desperate of prayers.

Using our usual method, read the passages three times slowly. Pray between readings: *Lord, open my eyes to the help you have given in the Scriptures. Clear my mind of distractions, and enable me to see and understand your words*. Note words or phrases that stand out to you on your final reading. I have written the passages out for you below.

Read Romans 8:26 and Hebrews 4:15-16.

> The Spirit also helps us in our weakness, because we do not know what to pray for as we should, but the Spirit himself intercedes for us with inexpressible groanings. (Romans 8:26)
>
> For we do not have a high priest who is unable to sympathize with our weaknesses, but one who has been tempted in every way as we are, yet without sin. Therefore, let us approach the throne of grace with boldness, so that we may receive mercy and find grace to help us in time of need. (Hebrews 4:15-16)

- What words or phrases stood out to you? Why?

- Psalm 12 says that God responds to the groaning of the needy. What makes groaning different from an articulate prayer?

- You and I groan under the weights we carry. We groan before we even have words to name our pain. We groan when words aren't enough. Have you had a time of suffering when you couldn't form words to name it or explain it? How were your prayers affected?

- How do you respond to the truth that God the Spirit groans with us?

The third principle that guides us in this study is that when we have no words, God gives us words through lament and stories of suffering in Scripture. Have you ever been in a session with a counselor or therapist and they named something you were experiencing that you couldn't quite explain on your own? It is powerful to have help to name what we are feeling or experiencing. And that is exactly what the Scriptures we are studying will do for us.

- What does it feel like when someone helps you name an emotion or struggle that you had a hard time explaining?

As we close this week, know that you do not suffer alone. *God is with you.* Hebrews 4:15 says that Jesus was tempted as we are, and he is not unaffected by our suffering. He, in fact, has made a way for us to bring our suffering to God's throne room, even when it is simply groaning too deep for words.

But God also—as the one who knows us best—offers us help through the Scriptures, to name what we are feeling, the sins against us, and the pain of its aftermath. Through naming our struggle and turning toward God in complaint, we find unexpected grace and mercy to see us through with hope.

Envision yourself in the throne room of God, and hear his words of grace and mercy to you from Psalm 12.

"Because of the devastation of the needy
and the groaning of the poor,
I will now rise up," says the LORD.
"I will provide safety for the one who longs for it."
The words of the LORD are pure words,
like silver refined in an earthen furnace,
purified seven times.
You, LORD, will guard us;
you will protect us from this generation forever.

Now sit before the Lord in prayer, without words if needed, knowing that you do not sit alone. The Holy Spirit groans with us. God is not unaffected by your suffering. He has not left you alienated to groan under the weight of this world alone.

WEEK TWO | AN OWL AMONG THE RUINS—PSALM 102

Group Session Introduction

In week one, we acknowledged the extensive ways the fall of humanity brought suffering to the world, our community, and our personal relationships. But what remains good? The bottom line is that God's character and purposes for his children remain unchanged. Scripture gives us hints

of this fact through the imagery of the tree of life and the Garden of Eden that extend from Genesis to Revelation in the Bible.

Watch this week's video.

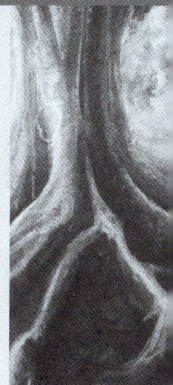

DISCUSSION

Read Genesis 2:8-12 together.

> The LORD God planted a garden in Eden, in the east, and there he placed the man he had formed. The LORD God caused to grow out of the ground every tree pleasing in appearance and good for food, including the tree of life in the middle of the garden, as well as the tree of the knowledge of good and evil.
>
> A river went out from Eden to water the garden. From there it divided and became the source of four rivers. The name of the first is Pishon, which flows through the entire land of Havilah, where there is gold. Gold from that land is pure; bdellium and onyx are also there.

Read Revelation 22:1-5 together.

> Then the angel showed me the river of the water of life, bright as crystal, flowing from the throne of God and of the Lamb through the middle of the street of the city; also, on either side of the river, the tree of life with its twelve kinds of fruit, yielding its fruit each month. The leaves of the tree were for the healing of the nations. No longer will there be anything accursed, but the throne of God and of the Lamb

will be in it, and his servants will worship him. They will see his face, and his name will be on their foreheads. And night will be no more. They will need no light of lamp or sun, for the Lord God will be their light, and they will reign forever and ever. (ESV)

- Compare the imagery of Revelation 22 to that of the Garden of Eden in Genesis 2. How are they the same or different?
- Describe a comforting location for you in nature. How does being there make you feel?
- For millennia throughout the world, people have cultivated both ornamental and fruitful gardens. Why do you think that practice has transcended time and culture?
- What kind of things do humans find satisfying about gardening or enjoyable in a garden cultivated by someone else?
- In Revelation 22, the tree of life is described as growing on both sides of a river that flows from the throne of God and the Lamb. What does that imagery imply to you?
- The Revelation passage refers to Jesus as "the Lamb." What is the significance of this name of Christ?
- "No longer will there be anything accursed." This is a powerful statement. What does this language from Revelation 22 communicate to you about the suffering you or your community have experienced?
- As John received Revelation 22, he was exiled on the island of Patmos for his beliefs about Jesus. Many other disciples, his good friends and companions in ministry, had been brutally murdered for their beliefs. How do you think this vision helped him persevere amid his trials?
- Revelation 22:4 says that we will see God's face. John had actually walked with Jesus face-to-face, but at the time he received this vision, he had not seen Jesus in person for at least forty years. What would it mean for him to see God face-to-face again?
- How does this final scene of human life in eternity help you interpret your or your community's suffering?

Humanity's fall resulted in pervasive suffering. Our external world and internal selves are deeply broken, and we groan under the weight of the consequences.

But what remains good? The fall did not touch God's character or his good plan for his children. As we close today, let's pray together that our eternal destiny laid out in Revelation 22 will help us interpret and endure the struggles we are facing now.

PSALM 102:1-11 — DAY 1

What does suffering feel like?

I have spent a lot of time numbing myself to suffering—slamming the door on my thoughts, going on walks, staring at the sky, shutting down my mind. Sometimes the only way to turn off troubling thoughts is to replace them with amusement, literally things that don't involve thinking. Movies, television, novels—I've used all of these to turn off thoughts and numb myself to pain I am experiencing. Many of us numb ourselves because the feelings of suffering can be suffocating and nauseating. But, at least for me, the numbness eventually wears off.

As tempting as it is, numbing doesn't actually heal our wounds. Often we have to feel what hurts in order to heal. The author of Psalm 102 is not numb to his suffering. He feels it emotionally and physically. His description of suffering is earthy and gritty. But he also reminds himself and us that all is not lost. As we reviewed in this week's video, God's character and his ultimate plan for us have not been lost. The truth of both our current pain and our future glory are intertwined in this psalm in helpful ways.

Today's reading articulates the psalmist's pain and stops before the affirmations of God's character and purposes. Read the verses through three times. Pray between each reading that God would open your mind to his help in this passage. Clear your mind of preconceived notions about this psalm at each reading. Finally, on the third reading, circle the words or phrases that stand out to you.

Read Psalm 102:1-11.

- What words or phrases stood out to you in this passage? Why?

- Did you notice in verse 1 the first thing that makes this a psalm of lament? The psalmist turns to God in his cry! How would you sum up his complaint in verses 1-11?

- In what ways can you identify with the psalmist's description of suffering?

The psalmist says he is like a lonely owl among ruins, a solitary bird on a rooftop. He's sitting in the devastated ruins of his life. His enemies ridicule him instead of having compassion on him. But most painful is the feeling that God has abandoned him: "You have picked me up and thrown me aside" (v. 10). Mark D. Futato says in his commentary on Psalms and Proverbs that "the psalmist was sick in heart as well as in body. And *he let nothing go unspoken in prayer.*"

- The psalmist cries out to God five times to listen and come to his aid. What five actions did the psalmist explicitly call on God to do? (Though some of the lines are worded passively, what are the actions they imply?)

- Have you called on God as boldly as this psalmist did? If so, what prompted you to cry out? And if not, what holds you back?

- If you have called on the Lord boldly, write out some of the circumstances that brought you to that point.

After the psalmist describes his suffering, he says stark words in verse 10: "You [God] have picked me up and thrown me aside." The image is of trash on a path that one throws away to get it out of their sight. This imagery resonates with me. It speaks to emotions many of us carry when we are in the middle of deep suffering.

- When have you felt like trash thrown or kicked out of the way, irrelevant to others—even to God—as everyone else goes on with their lives? Describe the circumstances surrounding those emotions.

The psalmist describes his days as numbered and quickly diminishing (vv. 3, 11). He feels temporary, as if his time is almost done. He would be dumped in a grave and left to decompose. Like trash.

- How have you come up against your own limitation of days?

- For those experiencing terminal illness, you have perhaps been given a literal time frame for your remaining days. How does the fleeting nature of life affect our outlook on the days we have left?

LORD, hear my prayer; let my cry for help come before you. Do not hide your face from me in my day of trouble. Listen closely to me; answer me quickly when I call.

PSALM 102:1-2

We end today's meditation at a sobering point. As we read on, there is hope and encouragement to be found in this psalm, but it is good for us to first face head-on the suffocating, nauseating feelings the psalmist describes. God invites us—exhorts us—to bring the reality of our suffering before him.

Would you make the psalmist's opening prayer in verses 1-2 your closing prayer today?

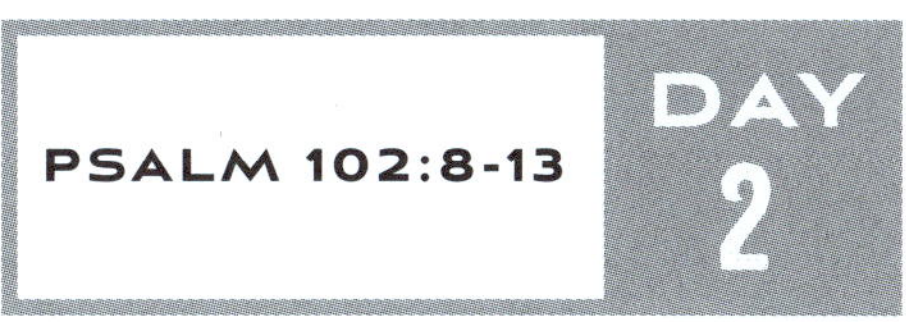

After all that was lost at humanity's fall, what remains good?

Today, we are going to start digging into the hope Psalm 102 provides. Hope does not negate the pain we feel. Consider the verse "Jesus wept" (John 11:35). In the story of Lazarus in John 11, Jesus had every hope that he would raise Lazarus from the dead, yet he still grieved at the suffering that sin had caused those he loved. Yet amid our grief, hope helps us put our pain in context. It equips us to persevere through the suffering.

Following our normal practice, pray that God would open your eyes to wonderful things in his Scriptures (Psalm 119:18). Then, read through the passage slowly three times. On your last reading, circle words or phrases that stand out to you.

Read Psalm 102:8-13.

- What words or phrases stood out to you in these verses? Why did they resonate with you?

The psalmist could not be any lower. He is isolated from his community and feels like God has discarded him as trash.

But you, Lord . . .

As I write these words, my eyes tear up so I can barely see my computer. I cry whenever I get to that amazing, hopeful word "but" in verse 12. The linking word *but* is a contrasting conjunction. It doesn't negate the first clause. Instead, it brings contrasting information to further flesh out the meaning of the first clause. The psalmist does not negate the physical pain and emotional isolation he is feeling. He adds to it though. He says, there are other facts to be considered. Like God in Revelation revealing to John what was going on behind the scenes of the tribulation of the church, the psalmist here tells us there are other truths at play that can help us understand our reality.

In particular, there are two major contrasts in today's reading.

- What is the contrast in verses 11 and 12?

- What is the contrast in verses 8, 10, and 13?

Even though he felt his days were numbered, the psalmist recognized that he was a part of an eternal story. God is enthroned forever. In Revelation 22, a crystal-clear river flowed from God's throne, nourishing the tree of life. The psalmist felt his death coming, the ultimate result of humanity's fall. But in the shade of the tree of life, the curse is no more. In the Eternal King who made that tree, the psalmist found lasting hope.

- Human or animal, personal or global, in what ways has death affected you?

The throne referenced in Psalm 102:12 and Revelation 22:3 symbolizes God's power. He is sovereign, and his purposes will stand. Through these references to God's throne, we have an important reminder of God's unchanging character. God is in control. He is on the throne. He is King of kings and Lord of lords. He was on his throne before humanity's fall, and he is still there now.

But God's sovereignty is insufficient, even terrifying, apart from other truths about him revealed in this psalm. There are a lot of strong, powerful leaders in control of their domains who are not safe people. Thankfully, we see a contrasting yet complementary trait in verse 13. God is also *compassionate*. The English word *compassion* comes from the Latin for suffering (*passio*); the prefix *com* means to enter into. *Compassio* in Latin means "to suffer with."

- How has God shown us his compassion? How has he suffered with us?

Our God is a sovereign, powerful king—one to be feared and obeyed. But he also loves and sacrifices for his people and promises to rescue them from all their suffering and shame. He entered our suffering and carried it with us, even *for* us.

We call this the Passion of the Christ—this suffering that Jesus took on in our place that we might be presented sinless to God. Jesus, God-incarnate (meaning God in the flesh with us), literally suffered with and for us. This is the gospel.

- How does it comfort you (or might it comfort you, if you are not quite to the point of accepting it for yourself) that God is both sovereign and compassionate?

The psalmist felt like trash, disposed of by God. But God's true view of the psalmist was very different from how the psalmist felt. The psalmist felt isolated. But God had compassion on him. He had not discarded him at all.

- Today, take time to reflect on the contrast between how you may feel and what God says is true about his character and his care for you. You don't need to fully reconcile these contrasts in your thoughts. Just write how you feel right now and follow it with Psalm 102's contrasting truth about God.

Now that you have noted the differences between what you feel and what God says is true, talk to God about those differences in prayer.

We have read several times now of how the psalmist felt discarded by God. We will continue to think about our feelings of isolation and irrelevance and how they contrast with the unchanging reality of God's character and purposes, with all that remains good.

On day two, we looked at God's sovereignty and compassion. Today, let's look at his good plan to secure for us flourishing life with him for eternity—plans that sin and Satan have failed to disrupt.

Using our usual practice, ask God to open your eyes to helpful truths in today's Scripture reading. Then read today's passage slowly three times. On your last reading, circle any words or phrases that stand out to you.

Read Psalm 102:11-17.

- What phrases did you circle today? Why did those phrases resonate with you?

We are going to focus on verse 13 today. "It is time to show favor to her," the psalmist says. "The appointed time has come." This is loaded language in the Scriptures that shows up throughout the psalms and into the New Testament. We study this phrase in more depth in week six, but it is worth a look now. I also go into this topic in my book *Companions in Suffering: Comfort for Times of Loss and Loneliness*, from which I draw on in this study.

First, the language of "a time of favor" implies a time of disfavor, does it not? At one point, the psalmist clearly felt out of favor with God. He said earlier he felt discarded by God like trash! That doesn't sound very favorable.

In my own journey through family mental illness, divorce, and cancer, I have struggled with feeling that I am out of favor with God. What did I do wrong to lose his favor? If I'm out of favor with God, why even bother trying to have a relationship with him? If I am out of favor with God, what does it matter if he has a good plan for everybody else? Am I even included in it?

- What circumstances have caused you or someone you love to feel out of God's favor?

- If you feel out of favor with God because of actual sin in your life, would you take time now to confess your sin to God?

Romans 8:1 reminds us there is no condemnation for those who are in Christ Jesus. God invites us to come to him and confess freely. Our compassionate God forgives (Psalm 78:38).

Looking back at Psalm 102:13, the language that we read is messianic—it alludes to Jesus as the Messiah. In 2 Corinthians 6:2, Paul uses this language that echoes Isaiah 49:8 to describe Jesus: "See, now is the acceptable time"—*the time of favor*—"now is the day of salvation!"

The time of favor and good will is upon all who believe in Christ's resurrection and confess him as Lord (Romans 10:9-10). How is a time of God's favor on us even as we groan under the weight of all that is broken in this world and our own lives? God's favor is on us because of Christ's death in our place.

Jesus has started us on a journey toward the day when our feelings will catch up with the reality of his favor on us. On that day, we will sit in the shade of the tree of life, and we will be nourished by the river that flows from the throne of the Lamb (Revelation 22:1-2).

How do you allow God's favor to break into a season of suffering? It starts by remembering "there is now no condemnation for those in Christ Jesus" (Romans 8:1). It starts by putting aside any self-condemnation you may feel for the path your life has taken.

- What shame or feelings of condemnation have you struggled with because of the suffering you have endured?

I've struggled with shame and self-condemnation again and again throughout my trials. Surely, I have thought, there must have been something more I could have done to avoid my divorce or cancer diagnosis. Was there more I could have done to fight off my loved one's mental illness? It is good and right that we confess our sins and own our mistakes. But in Christ we can put away self-condemnation. Through Christ's punishment in our place, God's eternal favor is secured for us.

Take time today to pray honestly about the contrast between how you feel in your suffering and what God says is true about you in Christ. Do you feel like his disfavor is on you? Do you feel self-condemnation? Bring those feelings to him today that you may find grace and mercy in your time of loneliness and isolation.

PSALM 102:16-22 — DAY 4

SUFFERING IS UNIVERSAL, yet it feels alienating. In Psalm 102, we are given a glimpse of community in the middle of deep suffering. The psalmist invites us to see our individual struggles in light of the struggles all God's people share: we are in the middle of a story that started in Eden in the shade of the tree of life and ends in a city with that same tree anchoring its landscape. We walk now in the valley of the shadow of death, but the shade of the tree of life is our destiny. God has not lost the storyline.

Today we will read and meditate on more of Psalm 102. Using our typical practice, ask God to open your eyes to beautiful truths in this passage. Then, read it slowly three times. On your last reading, circle words or phrases that stand out to you.

READ PSALM 102:16-22.

- What words or phrases did you note today? Why?

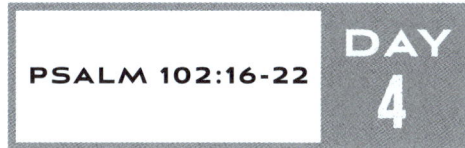

I love the certainty of verses 16 and 17. The Lord will rebuild Zion. The Lord will pay attention to the prayers of the desolate. I also love verse 18:

"This will be written for a later generation, and a people who have not yet been created will praise the Lord." That's you and me, and our children after us.

Psalm 102, written thousands of years ago, helps us find community in suffering today. The psalmist struggled with emotions many of us face, and he knew he was writing for those who would live long after him. Psalm 102 reminds us that we share the struggles of God's people in the Old Testament. We share in the Scriptures' larger story—in the story of Zion.

- In the Bible, Zion is identified as a hill in Jerusalem where the City of David was located (2 Samuel 5:7). Over time, the term came to reference the Temple or Jerusalem as a whole (Isaiah 10:12). God's children are even called the Daughters of Zion (Matthew 21:5). In the New Testament, the term's long-term meaning becomes clear. Look up Hebrews 12:22. What ultimately is Zion?

Hebrews and Revelation use *Zion* in a heavenly, eternal sense. But what relevance does a heavenly Zion have for us today? My grandfather used to say someone was "so heavenly minded, they're no earthly good." But that is not the case with this heavenly reality.

He looked down from his holy heights—
the Lord gazed out from heaven to earth—
to hear a prisoner's groaning,
to set free those condemned to die. (Psalm 102:19-20)

Zion may be an eternal, heavenly city, but its reality breaks into the here and now of our day-in, day-out struggles. The shade from the tree of life shelters us even now in the valley of the shadow of death. God looks down from the holy heights of Zion, and he hears our cries. He pays "attention to the prayer of the destitute," and he does not despise our cries to him (Psalm 102:17).

Do you need this encouragement today? God does not despise your prayers. He is paying attention. Know that our God, who suffers with us—and is sovereign over Satan, sin, and death—is listening. Cry out to him, for he cares.

- How does the truth that God does not despise our prayers, that he pays attention to the cries of the needy, change how you approach him?

To close today's study, read Luke 4:16-21 about Jesus proclaiming in the synagogue that he is the Messiah. Please don't skip this. It closes the loop between God's good plan that was not lost at the fall of man and the time of God's favor on us through Jesus.

- In closing, write out your prayer to God. Bring your fears, your shame, and your hopes to God, knowing that he hears you and his favor is on you because of Christ.

PSALM 102:19-28 DAY 5

PSALM 102 REMINDS US of what was not lost at the fall—God's love for his children and his undeniable plan to bring us back to him. It begins with a prayer that God would hear the psalmist's cries. The psalmist then spells out his despair. But he is assured of God's compassion. Though our suffering feels alienating, God the Son entered into it, and he sits with us in it.

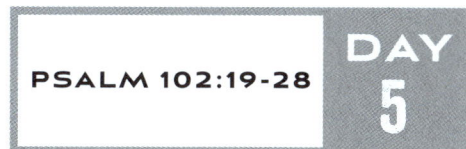

To reinforce this reality, Psalm 102 turns messianic in its allusions to Jesus. On day three, we read language of the appointed time of God's favor and discovered that this time is now upon us in Christ (2 Corinthians 6:2). On day four, we read from Luke 4 that Jesus claimed to be the one who released the captives and rescued those who are oppressed. Today's final section of Psalm 102 is messianic as well, though it may not first appear that way.

We will better understand this section of Psalm 102 if we consider the first chapter of Hebrews; it quotes Psalm 102 in a set of Old Testament quotations related to Jesus Christ. Here's how the author of Hebrews begins this set of quotations:

> Long ago God spoke to our ancestors by the prophets at different times and in different ways. In these last days, he has spoken to us by his Son. God has appointed him heir of all things and made the universe through him. The Son is the radiance of God's glory and the exact expression of his nature, sustaining all things by his powerful word. After making purification for sins, he sat down at the right hand of the Majesty on high. (Hebrews 1:1-3)

Now, read today's verses three times slowly using our usual method. Between each reading, pray for God to open your eyes to new things in his word. Circle words or phrases on your last reading that grab your attention.

Read Psalm 102:19-28.

- Knowing how Hebrews uses this chapter to point to Jesus, what words or phrases did you circle? What did they communicate to you about Jesus?

These verses are full of contrasts. "Perish," "wear out," and "pass away" on the one hand. "Never ending," "established," and "secure" on the other. Our suffering is part of the decay brought into the world through humanity's fall. There is much that is fleeting in our lives. Yet Jesus endures. Jesus is the same. His years will never end.

- Verse 28 finally brings us back into the picture. Where do we land in the spectrum between decay and eternal life according to this verse?

God's character and his purposes for us have not changed. Though the psalmist initially felt like trash, discarded by God, *he ended the psalm knowing he and his children will be established, the very opposite of being disposable.* They would dwell securely in Christ, who remains the same, unchanged by humanity's fall.

As we close this week's study, let this psalm of lament plant in your heart seeds of hope. God is on his throne, and he has compassion on you. He is not dispassionate toward your struggles. Furthermore, he knows what he is doing, and he will accomplish his plans. He will establish us securely under the shade of the tree of life, watered by the river that flows from his throne. There will be no tears and no regrets. This is our destiny.

Personalize the following excerpts from Psalm 102 in prayer to your unchanging Savior whose character and purposes still stand.

Lord, hear my prayer;
let my cry for help come before you.
Do not hide your face from me in my day of trouble.

[You] will pay attention to the prayer of the destitute
and will not despise their prayer.
This will be written for a later generation,
and a people who have not yet been created will praise the Lord.

You are the same,
and your years will never end.
Your servants' children will dwell securely,
and their offspring will be established before you.

WEEK THREE | DARKNESS IS MY ONLY FRIEND—PSALM 88

Group Session Introduction

In week one, we defined groaning and lament in Scripture, and we saw that we do not groan alone. In week two, we looked at God's unchanging character and purpose that still hold us fast despite all that was lost at the fall. Through the psalms of lament, Scripture models intertwined grief and hope, the last not negating the necessity of the first.

This week, we will sit in Scripture's examples of grief and groaning again with the author of Psalm 88 and Job. Both give us language for emotions we may not want to admit we feel. Note that this will be a heavy week, studying a heavy psalm. Even so, there is grace to be experienced through it.

Watch this week's video.

DISCUSSION

Read together Job's lament, which actually sounds more like an accusation.

> If I have sinned, what have I done to you,
> Watcher of humanity?
> Why have you made me your target,
> so that I have become a burden to you? (Job 7:20)

> God hands me over to the unjust;
> he throws me to the wicked.
> I was at ease, but he shattered me;
> he seized me by the scruff of the neck
> and smashed me to pieces.
> He set me up as his target;
> his archers surround me.
> He pierces my kidneys without mercy
> and pours my bile on the ground.

He breaks through my defenses again and again;
he charges at me like a warrior. (Job 16:11-14)

This week, we will see that the very God whom Job accused of bringing about all his suffering is the same God who met Job in his lament and slowly transformed him.

- Where do you go with the hard things in life? Are you someone who quickly goes to God in prayer; do you try several other things before resorting to prayer; or do you tend to avoid praying about the hard stuff?
- Why is expressing dark emotions so hard as a Christian?
- What are some of Job's accusations against God?
- Consider Job's tone with God. Are you encouraged by how freely Job speaks to God? Or are you affronted that he talked to God like that?
- What situations, generally or specific to your life or community, prompt the kind of questions, even accusations, of God that Job had?
- What kinds of things feel off-limits or risky to bring to God?
- Have you felt "antsy anxiety" (as described in the video)? How did it manifest in your mind and body?
- If you have had a time when you felt like you needed Scripture but could not bring yourself to read it, what was helpful to you?
- If you have a friend struggling this way, what practical things can you do (more than say) to come alongside them?

God preserved language for us in his eternal Word to help us bring our darkest thoughts and feelings to God's throne room. Along with Psalm 88, we have a road map for bringing dark emotions to God in the book of Job. Though Job's friends accused him of evil, Job knew he was innocent, and he lamented injustice as injustice. Job called evil evil, and his eternally preserved words equip us to name our struggles and articulate the pain and disillusionment we endure.

Theologian R. W. L. Moberly writes about lament in the *New International Dictionary of Old Testament Theology and Exegesis*:

> The predominance of laments at the very heart of Israel's prayers means that the problems that give rise to lament are not something marginal or unusual but rather are central to the life of faith. . . . Moreover they show that the experience of anguish and puzzlement in the life of faith is not a sign of deficient faith, something to be outgrown or put behind one, but rather is intrinsic to the very nature of faith.

Let's pray together that our study this week helps us find language to bring our darkest thoughts boldly to God in our time of need.

PSALM 88:1-9 **DAY 1**

THIS WEEK WE WILL LOOK at what many consider the darkest psalm, Psalm 88, as well as a dark story of pain and loss in the life of Job. Psalm 88 is the only psalm that does not resolve in some way. It ends, "Darkness is my only friend." Why should we spend a week in such despairing Scripture?

Because lament is a means of God's grace.

Biblical lament is a supernatural, mysterious thing. God's Spirit through God's Word helps us bring our darkest thoughts directly to God's throne room. He hears our cries to him, and he promises grace and help that is beyond our ability to rationally imagine.

"When [the psalms] speak of fear and hope, they use such words that no painter could so depict for your fear or hope and no Cicero or other orator has so portrayed them," Martin Luther says in his *Word and Sacrament*. "And that they speak these words to God and with God, this I repeat, is the best thing of all."

Pray that Psalm 88 would help you cry out to God with emotions and needs that you do not even know how to name. Then slowly read the beginning of the psalm three times. As you read, slow yourself to contemplate the psalmist's language and note any phrases you identify with.

READ PSALM 88:1-9.

- What words or phrases did you note in your reading?

- How do the phrases you noted articulate emotions and realities you have had a hard time putting into words—or have been afraid to put into words to God?

- Each time I read this psalm, I am struck with the agency the psalmist assigns to God for his suffering. Write out the psalmist's accusations of God from verses 6-8.

- What accusations have you or others around you felt or spoken toward God?

- It is hard to intuit the psalmist's tone in verses 6-8. Do you think the psalmist is angry when he says these things to God? Confused? Something else? What tone do you hear when you read his words?

Note the contrast of the first line, "LORD, God of my salvation," and verse 7, "Your wrath weighs heavily on me." This contrast is painful. *Salvation* and *wrath* are antonyms. They are not supposed to exist together. The psalmist articulates emotional and spiritual whiplash. Like a child who receives a present from one hand of a parent and a backhand across the face with the other hand.

- In light of what we studied in week two on God's sovereignty and his compassion, suffering can be deeply confusing. This God who saves me—must I also implore him to hear me? This God who saves me—why does it feel like he's punishing me? How have you or a loved one experienced spiritual and emotional whiplash?

There is no lecture in this psalm. Though we know God is sovereign, compassionate, and wise, he does not instruct us in how to feel or give us answers for our own desperate moments. Instead, Psalm 88 is a prayer. With this psalm, God gives us a tool to live out the words we read in Hebrews 4:16: "Therefore, let us approach the throne of grace with boldness, so that we may receive mercy and find grace to help us in *time of need*" (emphasis mine).

God's compassion and wisdom, though not mentioned in this psalm, are at the heart of why this psalm was recorded in Scripture and kept for the ages. In your time of need, your time of confusion, your feelings of whiplash and dissonance between who you thought God was and what your circumstances proclaim him to be, God guides you to approach him boldly and articulate to him clearly: "I am desperate."

- Write your own prayer to God in light of disorienting circumstances in your life or your community's life. Use Psalm 88:1-9 as a guide.

DAY 2 — PSALM 88:9-18

The psalmist in Psalm 88 is tired of crying out to God. But God preserved his words in Scripture, and they are a helpful guide for those of us who identify with the psalmist—who have brought our cries to God, while God seemed silent or uncaring or even outright hostile in response.

Pray now that God would minister grace to you as you read the last half of Psalm 88 today. Then read the passage three times slowly, noting words or phrases on your last reading that reflect your own feelings and fears.

Read Psalm 88:9-18.

- How does the language of this passage reflect your own fears and questions of God?

- Most of us have had a season of praying to God in which it seemed God rejected our prayers. How did that affect you emotionally and spiritually?

- Describe the confusion the psalmist articulates in verses 10-12.

The suffering of those who put their faith in God does not seem to make God look good or to bring God glory. Prosperity of the righteous, we think, makes God look better than the suffering of those who follow him.

The psalmist seems to have no concept of anything happening outside of life on earth, and it's hard to fault him. Once death comes and this life ends, he feels the purpose of his life is over. But the first chapters of the book of Job tell us there is more going on outside of our line of vision, as Satan and God have a discussion about Job in the heavenly realm. The psalmist can't envision, amid his suffering, anything going on outside his immediate circumstances.

- I count at least four actions in verses 13-18 that the psalmist feels God is doing to him. Write them out below.

This psalm does not resolve. It does not turn to hope. It simply records a wounded sufferer's tormented questions of God. Why are you doing this? Why don't you answer me? If you are who you say you are, God, none of this makes sense to me!

- Scripture says these psalms were inspired by God and kept by him in the Scriptures for our help (2 Timothy 3:16-17). Why do you think God inspired and kept this psalm for you today?

- To close today, would you write out your questions of God as the psalmist did and bring them to God in prayer?

"Darkness is my only friend."

Psalm 88 leaves us sitting in the reality of our suffering. It does not pressure us into quick answers or easy resolution to our suffering. Instead, it models naming our struggles honestly to God.

In the quintessential story of suffering in Scripture, the story of Job, we also see a man who is brutally honest with God about his internal struggle. What happened between him and God is mysterious. Job was transformed as he poured out his grief; his brutal lament became a means of God's grace to him. You can see as the chapters progress in the book of Job that long before his outward circumstances change, Job's inner turmoil is transformed.

Many Bible scholars believe Job's story was the first part of Scripture to be written down. In the story, Satan accuses Job of only obeying God because God has been good to him. But God says Job follows him because God is God, not only because God is good. The subsequent trial of Job is ultimately a trial of God—is God worthy of worship for his character alone? Job becomes the primary witness.

Satan attacks Job's family in Job 1. He attacks his body in Job 2. The Bible does not tell us how long it took for Job to speak in chapter three, but when he does, his words are raw and brutal. God preserves this language of lament for us in his eternal Word and notes that Job did not sin in his cries to God. God would eventually correct Job's characterization of him as unjust, but God never condemned Job for the manner in which he cried out.

As you read today, ask God to help you recognize emotions that you or someone you love has faced in grief. As is our practice, read this portion of Job slowly three times. On your last reading, note phrases or words that stand out to you.

READ JOB 3:20-26.

- Which of Job's words or phrases stood out to you? In what ways do you identify with them?

Job was in a dark place, desiring death as a welcome relief to his suffering. He was agitated, unable to rest or relax, and without a hope in the world.

Verse 25 hits me each time I read it: what Job feared and dreaded overtook him. This language helped me articulate my own griefs. I remember the fear and dread I experienced as mental illness and then divorce began their slow but steady march toward my family. I could see their looming shadows and dreaded their pending destruction. I tried to defend my family against them, yet I could not stop their progress. What I feared overtook and seemed to destroy my family.

- Think of a time when something you feared overtook you or a loved one. Describe the situation and how it affected you emotionally and spiritually.

- Job's words, particularly verses 25-26, gave me language for the years of anxiety I felt when those destructive shadows stalked and overtook my family. Job gives a compelling description of anxiety and dread. How has anxiety manifested in your life and body?

We are not alone in the "antsy anxiety" we feel when, like a prisoner, we shake at the bars due to the trials God has allowed in our life. Job's words have been a sweet blessing to me when I experience anxiety that refuses to let me rest. Without condemnation, God preserved in his Scriptures the words of another who felt the same anxiety I feel, who paced long before I was born. His lament helps me formulate my own.

- In closing today, write your prayer to God. Spell out your questions to God and any anxiety you feel about your (or a loved one's) circumstances. It is normal if your prayer sounds like one you wrote out this week or last; we may not get past these emotions in an hour, a week, or even the duration of this study. But God gives us his grace day-by-day, hour-by-hour, as we bring these dark emotions again and again to him.

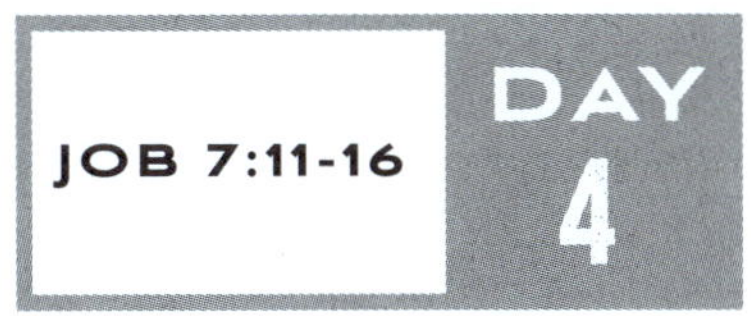

Job, like the author of Psalm 88, puts to words emotions and questions we may feel we cannot bring to God in prayer. God hasn't left us alone to figure out deep suffering. He is compassionate. He is with us in our suffering, and the Scriptures give evidence of how he cares and guides us through it.

In the book of Job, Job's questions and complaints—interspersed with the unhelpful responses of his friends—take up thirty-five chapters before God finally speaks to him.

We are going to read two passages today. Ask God to open your eyes and help you through each Scripture passage. On your last reading, note words or phrases that stand out to you. First we will read Job's complaint slowly three times.

Read Job 7:11-16.

- Job describes his feelings of life's futility and vanity from multiple angles. What phrases did you note? Why did they stand out to you?

- What circumstances have caused you to feel that your efforts in life have been futile?

- Did you notice in this passage that even the bed is not comforting to Job? Instead, it is just another form of torment for him. When you are suffering, is sleep a help or a struggle? What things plague you when you try to sleep?

In the previous verses of this chapter that we didn't read, Job said he is like a hired worker with no control over his own existence. His only allotment is months of vanity and nights of trouble (v. 3). He feels like a mere cog in God's wheel.

I can identify. As my marriage fell apart, I wondered, "What was the point of all I did to help build a stable, Christian family if it all could be taken away despite my best efforts?" When everything we've built is swept away, we struggle to engage again.

Read verse 11 again.

Therefore I will not restrain my mouth.
I will speak in the anguish of my spirit;
I will complain in the bitterness of my soul.

Like Job, I have had many times when I could not restrain my mouth or fake what I thought a good Christian sufferer should say and do. My problem comes when I vent those feelings to friends or family, particularly if my venting involves tearing others down. Job was written to comfort sufferers, not condemn them for imperfect words. And the implied invitation here is to vent these hard emotions to God himself. It is not gossip or slander if we cry it out to God in prayer. God's throne room is the ultimate safe place to vent our raw emotions and struggles when there is no other place to go.

- Have you had a time when you or your loved ones could not restrain your words, when you gave full vent to your anguish or bitterness? How can venting to God help you refrain from venting to others in a way that tears down or slanders?

In verse 16, Job says, "I give up! I will not live forever. Leave me alone, for my days are a breath." This is a hard verse, but I can identify with Job's anguish and frustration. When I was first diagnosed with breast cancer after my divorce, I broke when I read this verse. It articulated a fear I could not put into words. I had followed God for most of my life, but now it felt like I would be better off without him—just leave me alone, God. What does a Christian do with that dark, depressing thought?

Bring it to God.

- What frustrations have you felt toward God? Name them here and bring them honestly to God right now.

As Job endures through the book, his lament also changes. In chapter 9, Job asks, "How can a man be justified before God?" (v. 2). God is not a man who Job can take to court (v. 32); there is no mediator who can settle matters between God and Job (v. 33). After all, this is God that Job's wrestling with.

Yet the God Job accused of bringing all manner of evil upon him is the same God who meets him in his lament and slowly transforms him. Lament was a means of God's grace to Job. And slowly, Job's lament began to transform.

This brings us to our second passage for today. We close with Job's words from Job 19, which you may recognize from Christian hymns and praise choruses. Read this passage through three times as in our usual practice.

READ JOB 19:25-27.

But I know that my Redeemer lives,
and at the end he will stand on the dust.
Even after my skin has been destroyed,
yet I will see God in my flesh.
I will see him myself;
my eyes will look at him, and not as a stranger.
My heart longs within me.

Job didn't know the name Jesus, and the concept of the Messiah had not yet been presented in any detail in Scripture. Nevertheless, as Job's lament progresses, he confesses belief that one lives who will reconcile him with God. This Redeemer will stand where Job cannot, allowing Job to see God face-to-face. Here we see Job's first true glimmer of hope. We now know that this language of a Redeemer is fulfilled in Christ (Titus 2:14).

We are not strangers to God, nor is he one to us. You are not wrestling with a stranger as you lament. You are wrestling with your Father, as Job did and as David did. Job's movement from utter despair—"I wish I had never been born!"—to hope amid pain is powerful.

- As we close today, take time to meditate on Job's words "I know my Redeemer lives." Each word here has meaning. Meditate on each word individually and then the statement as a whole. *I. Know. My. Redeemer. Lives.* Write out your reflections. Then personalize your words to God in prayer.

THIS WEEK, WE HAVE READ PSALM 88 and several passages from the book of Job. Job uses much more language amid his suffering than what we have read so far. If you feel stuck in your own antsy anxiety, I encourage you to listen to the book of Job on an audio Bible. Listen to Job's complaint on repeat until you, too, are ready to hear God speak as Job eventually was. Job's language is a gift from our wise and compassionate God. It helps us name our struggles and bring them to his throne of grace where we will find help in our time of need.

Now brace yourself. It's time for us to hear God speak to Job out of the whirlwind.

We don't know how long Job's complaints and questions went on before God finally spoke to him in Job 38. As I have said before, I went to Job's laments multiple times when I was at my worst state emotionally after my cancer diagnosis—I sat in the laments a while before I was ready to hear God's response. Job's laments, and my own that echoed his words, were a means of grace that moved me to the place where I could hear from God. I hope that you have sensed God's grace through your own laments readying your heart to hear God too.

When God speaks to Job, his words are good, they are helpful. But they are definitely not what we might think God should say to a righteous man who has suffered much.

Pray for God to open your eyes to his help in this passage, then read it through three times slowly.

Read Job 38:1-13.

- What is your initial response to God's words to Job?

- I expected God to say something more comforting to Job—at least as I define comfort. Write out a verse from Scripture that you find comforting. How does this passage differ?

I love Romans 8:28—the promise that God works all things together for our good. And Philippians 1:6 that gives the promise that God will finish the good work he started in us. I love the language of God as a strong refuge we find in Proverbs 14:26. But God said nothing like that to Job here.

- Instead, when he speaks to the quintessential sufferer in all of Scripture, God asks, "Where were you when I created the world?" God emphasizes his sovereign power, authority, and wisdom, but not his compassion. Why do you think God spoke that way to Job? How might these words be helpful to a sufferer?

God continues on this way for four chapters. "I am God, Job! I hung the stars in the sky, created the oceans and every animal in them. I am all powerful and all knowing." These are counterintuitive words of comfort. They flow counter to what our instincts think should comfort Job. At first, they may not seem comforting at all. Despite our first reaction, these words were actually helpful to Job. And they can be helpful to us.

In between cancer surgeries, I finally listened to Job 38 on my audio Bible. Outside in the dark, on a clear night on the farm, Orion's belt and other constellations God mentions in his response to Job shone brightly in the night sky. I hung my head in submission as I listened to God. I had to admit, "You are God, and I am not." But this submission to the sovereign God who created the universe wasn't one of humiliated defeat. It was a different kind of letting go. As I acknowledged my limitations, I could finally rest in God's power. After all, where else could I go? In that submission, I found deep comfort.

Are you able to find a space at night where you can see the stars clearly? If so, listen to the entire chapter of Job 38 under the shimmer of the constellations. Receive the comfort that God is God, and you are not. Believe that your Redeemer lives, and that through him God's love for you is eternally secure. You can be confident that all will be made right. The tree of life, lost at Eden, will be the tree you sit under for eternity.

- Write out your response to Job 38 below. Ask God to comfort you through his power and sovereign hand over circumstances in the world at large and your life in particular.

WEEK FOUR | MY FEET NEARLY SLIPPED—PSALM 73

Group Session Introduction

This week, we will meditate on Psalm 73. It is a case study in how to apply Hebrews 4:16, the theme of this Bible study. In Psalm 73, the psalmist Asaph enters God's sanctuary in a time of deep need, and he finds grace

and mercy that changes his entire perspective. As we read the chapter this week, we will get to witness the grace he receives through lament.

Watch this week's video.

DISCUSSION

In our group discussion, let's think deeply about Hebrews 4:16 as we prepare to work through Psalm 73 individually during our daily studies. First, Hebrews 4:16 isn't a stand-alone thought, so we have to back up one verse. Read these verses together.

> For we do not have a high priest who is unable to sympathize with our weaknesses, but one who has been tempted in every way as we are, yet without sin. Therefore, let us approach the throne of grace with boldness, so that we may receive mercy and find grace to help us in time of need. (Hebrews 4:15-16)

- What do you think the author means when he says Jesus sympathizes with our weaknesses?
- In week two, we studied God's *compassion*, which we learned was from the Latin phrase for "suffering with." The word *sympathy* is based on similar parts of speech in Greek. How might Jesus' sympathy and God's compassion overlap? What do these similar words communicate to you about God, including God the Son?
- What do you think the author of Hebrews means by "weaknesses"? What kind of weaknesses do you or your community experience?

- How does Jesus' sympathy with your weaknesses motivate you to come boldly before God's throne of grace?
- God is the King of the universe, yet his throne is described as a "throne of grace." Why do you think the author of Hebrews called it a "throne of *grace*" rather than a "throne of *power*"?
- Think of a time when you felt ashamed or unworthy of praying to God. How might Hebrews 4:15 have helped your perspective during that season?
- The author of Hebrews says we receive mercy and find grace in our time of need. What does that phrase "in our time of need" communicate to you about prayer?
- Mercy and grace are similar but different. Mercy is not receiving what we deserve (thus, not receiving punishment for sin), and grace is receiving something we don't deserve (thus, receiving forgiveness and help). Why do we need both grace and mercy in our time of need?
- When have you or your community needed mercy? How in the past has God shown mercy?
- How has God shown you, or your community, grace?

Lament is a necessary first response to this world's wrongs. It allows us to name our struggles against sin and suffering (including our own sin and the suffering we may have caused) and face head-on the consequences of humanity's fall in our lives. And there is help to be had through lament itself. In week three, we saw Job's movement from despair to hope. In Psalm 73, Asaph moves from despair to supernatural hope as well. How does Psalm 73 inform our own cycles of lament? How does it help us face and move forward amid our ongoing suffering and grief? These are some of the questions we will look at this week.

As we close, let's pray that God would help each of us believe there is tangible help for us when we come to God boldly in our time of need.

Thank God now for the grace and mercy he promises to minister to us as we come to him this week.

DAY 1
PSALM 73:1-12

MUCH OF OUR SUFFERING is due to the sickness and death that came into the world when humanity fell. But our suffering often involves harmful relationships as well. We suffer at the hand of others who lack compassion or sympathy, who harm without a care about the pain left in their wake.

Psalm 73 tells us of Asaph, a musician in God's temple, who wrestled deeply with the disconnect between what he believed about God in theory and what he witnessed around him in his circumstances. Asaph saw evil men getting away with harming others. He was grieved by the pride of the wicked and the harm they had done to his neighbors, and he cried out to God for understanding and help. For many of us, this will be a relatable psalm.

We will start today reading part of Psalm 73. Following our usual method, ask God to open your eyes to the helpful truth in his Scripture. Then, read the passage slowly three times, praying again between each reading. On your third reading, note words or phrases that resonate with you.

READ PSALM 73:1-12.

- What words or phrases stood out to you? How do you identify with Asaph's anguish and frustration?

- Did you notice the disconnect between verse 1 and the rest of the passage? What does the psalmist believe about God in theory? What are the circumstances around him that challenge his belief?

- Asaph says his feet nearly slipped, his steps nearly went astray. Think of a time you or a loved one have been on a precipice like he describes. What circumstances led you to feel that you were on the edge of slipping from the faith?

- Asaph sees the prosperity of the wicked. In verses 4-5, Asaph explains what he means when he says the wicked are prospering. How does he describe their prosperity?

The wicked challenged Asaph's understanding of the value of following God. We discussed in week two how suffering challenges our longing for a time of favor with God. Let's explore this common struggle a bit more.

Across the world—from Africa to Asia to North America—evangelicalism seems dominated by the teaching that when Christians make good choices in their life of faith, this results in good outcomes, in winning at life. Though the details can differ, the foundational belief is eerily similar—that if we obey God wholeheartedly, our church and life will flourish in visible and material ways, or at least we will have better outcomes than those who reject God and disobey him. This teaching shows up in different forms through various denominations and non-denominational groups.

- Consider how you may have experienced this prosperity gospel. Perhaps others have insinuated that if you had more faith, your suffering would resolve. Or if you just hold on a little longer, everything will turn out all right. What pressures have you felt from others who believe some form of the prosperity gospel?

- When the prosperity gospel is taken to its extreme, it undermines the testimony of sufferers, martyrs, and sacrificial servants in Christ's body. Most of all, it undermines the testimony of Christ. Consider Mark 8:31-35. In what ways does Christ's life and teaching challenge the prosperity gospel?

- The prosperity gospel, even in its subtle versions, bears terrible fruit. It alienates suffers from the church, and it makes them feel alienated from God. If we have adopted a form of the prosperity gospel, our belief system will be threatened when a fellow believer has ongoing suffering. We may even think we can avoid similar suffering in our own lives by casting blame on the sufferer or by insinuating they have caused the hardship. In what ways have you seen other sufferers blamed for bringing their suffering on themselves? Why do you think others wanted to blame them?

When we suffer, how do we endure in a church culture that responds to suffering with a prosperity gospel that makes it seem as if the sufferer brought their struggles on themselves? How can sufferers persevere with the church if they were betrayed or directly harmed by fellow Christians? And how do we reconcile our experience with the God we think blesses those who follow him? These are the questions Asaph faced in Psalm 73.

- Asaph is vexed because the wicked are flourishing, not the righteous. Why does prosperity follow the wicked? Perhaps Asaph was thinking along the lines of modern, western notions of karma, that good comes to those who do good, and evil comes to those who are wicked. In what ways have modern notions of karma shaped how you or those around you think about suffering and struggles in your life?

In Psalm 73:6-9, Asaph describes the character of the wicked in their prosperity.

Pride is their necklace,
and violence covers them like a garment.
Their eyes bulge out from fatness;
the imaginations of their hearts run wild.
They mock, and they speak maliciously;
they arrogantly threaten oppression.
They set their mouths against heaven,
and their tongues strut across the earth.

- How have you experienced a version of these descriptions in your own life, or the life of someone close to you? You don't have to answer them all, but pick one or two that feel particularly relevant to your experience.

Verses 10-11 are the saddest portion of this passage for me. I identify with them well. Asaph says that God's people turn toward the wicked and *drink in their overflowing words*. If you have experienced harm from wicked people, it is especially demoralizing when those in your life are persuaded to believe the wicked over the righteous.

- If you have experienced a situation when you or a loved one felt betrayed by family, friends, or fellow believers, perhaps the result of a family disagreement or church hurt, write how you were harmed emotionally and spiritually.

Close today's study by lifting those feelings of betrayal, abandonment, or confusion over the prosperity of the wicked to the Lord. Bring any of these demoralizing experiences to God's throne. Ask God to help you sift through karma, the prosperity gospel, and true belief in God as he shows himself in the Bible. You will find grace and mercy at his throne of grace for your time of need.

DAY 2 PSALM 73:13-16

In the reading of Psalm 73 on day one, Asaph wrestled with the prosperity of the wicked. In today's reading, he raises a question with which many sufferers can identify. Following our usual practice, read today's passage slowly three times. Between each reading, ask God to speak to you through his written Word. On the last reading, note words or phrases with which you particularly identify.

Read Psalm 73:13-16.

- Have you asked the question Asaph asks in verse 13? What circumstances in your life, or a loved one's life, have caused you to question whether following God is empty, vain, or meaningless?

In verse 15, Asaph says that if he had verbalized these things out loud, he would have betrayed God's people. Since we are reading Psalm 73 today, it is clear that Asaph eventually spoke his doubts publicly. But there was a point when he kept his questions inside, afraid he would betray God's people by giving voice to his despair over wicked people's prosperity and the seeming meaninglessness of obeying God.

After my divorce and breast cancer diagnosis, three different Christians came to me with their own crises of faith over my circumstances. Each had known me as a leader in the local church. They knew about the hardships I had endured through my divorce. They could not reconcile the new circumstances I was facing with what they believed about God. I could not tell them all the ways my cancer diagnosis was challenging my own faith; their faith was already weak. In those moments, I feared that speaking my own doubts aloud would have made faith harder for them. "If I had decided to say these things aloud, I would have betrayed your people" (v. 15).

- Think of a time when your internal faith was challenged but you felt you could not let anyone know, when you had to be strong for others—even faking it on the outside—in order not to challenge someone else's faith. What were you feeling internally? Why did you feel you couldn't say it out loud?

Many sufferers have reached the point in their own wrestling with God that Asaph reached in verse 16—hopeless. This word could also be translated as "troublesome" or "toil." In other words, when the wicked prospered, it bogged down Asaph's faith while he tried to figure out why. Their prosperity and God's goodness felt like too much to try to reconcile. When we are already emotionally exhausted, it can feel hopeless to try to understand what God is doing in our lives or our loved one's lives, just as it did for Asaph.

- When you have felt hopeless for yourself or a loved one, how did your mind and body respond?

Wrestling with God while receiving no answers to your questions is exhausting. Asaph felt hopeless, and his feet were close to slipping (v. 2). But as he sat exhausted and unable to figure out life on his own, God held Asaph fast. Though he was slipping, there was an unseen, unfelt tether that kept him from falling to his spiritual death.

For us too, though we may be exhausted, even hopeless, if we are in Christ, our faith is held fast by God. He holds us when we cannot hold ourselves. Read through this affirmation of your security in God from 1 Peter 1:3-5:

> Blessed be the God and Father of our Lord Jesus Christ. Because of his great mercy he has given us new birth into a living hope through the resurrection of Jesus Christ from the dead and into an inheritance that is imperishable, undefiled, and unfading, kept in heaven for you. You are being guarded by God's power through faith for a salvation that is ready to be revealed in the last time.

- Rest today. You do not have to have the answers. You do not have to reconcile the unreconcilable circumstances in your life. Asaph, one of God's conduits who wrote God's eternal words for us, struggled as you do. You can pray honestly as Asaph did in this psalm. Simply write out or pray aloud to God about your exhaustion.

Today, we reach the climax of Psalm 73 as Asaph recounts entering the sanctuary of God. In the week two video, I talked about the garden imagery in the tabernacle and temple. The lampstand, with its branches and flowers, was a golden reminder of the tree of life. The temple, with its carved palm trees and blossoms, echoed the floral design of the Garden of Eden. The sanctuary Asaph entered was a symbolic reminder of the peace and flourishing God meant for us to enjoy with him in perfection.

Before reading today's passage, ask God to open your eyes to beautiful and helpful truths in his Scriptures. As you read the first two times, imagine what it would have been like for the psalmist to enter the beauty of the temple. Then, on your third reading, note words or phrases that stand out to you.

READ PSALM 73:14-20.

- What words or phrases did you note? Why did these words stand out to you?

When Asaph enters the sanctuary, it is like God takes off Asaph's dirty, out-of-focus glasses and replaces them with the right prescription. Asaph can suddenly see clearly.

- What was the first thing that changed about Asaph's perspective when he entered God's sanctuary?

Previously, Asaph was vexed by how the wicked prospered. He envied them because it seemed that they didn't have the same troubles that the righteous had. They could mock God's people and speak poorly of God himself, but they prospered anyway. Now, Asaph has new glasses on, and he sees the wicked differently.

- What was Asaph's new understanding of the wicked who had taunted him and harmed others around him?

Years ago, the husband of a dear friend of mine left her for another woman. It was a deep betrayal, leaving my friend bankrupt and with young children to care for. I remember when, by God's grace, my friend's perspective about her ex-husband began to change, as genuine concern for his soul replaced bitterness over his betrayal. Like Asaph, she came to understand his destiny if he continued to walk away from God. By God's grace, her feelings of betrayal faded as she began to pray for his repentance.

In today's reading, Asaph moved from envying the wicked to awareness of the terrible destiny awaiting their souls. This transformation—a supernatural change of heart—is the kind of change only God can make.

In the Sermon on the Mount, Jesus tells us, "Love your enemies and pray for those who persecute you, so that you may be children of your Father in heaven" (Matthew 5:44-45).

- Who has harmed you or a loved one? Who has seemed to prosper despite their wickedness toward others? Would you bring their name to God today? Ask God to give you an eternal perspective on them as a person. Then ask God to move them to repent, for their destiny apart from him is sure.

PSALM 73:16-24

DAY 4

WHEN ASAPH ENTERED GOD'S SANCTUARY, God gave him new lenses to see his reality clearly. The first change was his perspective on his enemies. In today's reading, we will see that Asaph's perspective on himself changed as well.

Following our customary pattern, ask God, "Open my eyes so that I may contemplate wondrous things from your instruction" (Psalm 119:18). Then read the passage slowly three times. Discipline yourself to take it all in at once, waiting until the third reading to focus on any one phrase or verse. On your last reading, note the words or phrases that stand out to you.

READ PSALM 73:16-24.

- What words or phrases stood out as you read?

- What did Asaph come to understand about himself after he entered God's sanctuary?

In the video for this week, I talked about the self-condemnation I have felt through my life, and how I have needed God's affirmations again and again to calm my mind and give me confidence in him. Often, I condemned myself for unwarranted things out of my control. But sometimes, my self-condemnation *was* warranted. I am a sinner, and I have at times harmed others.

Asaph too had not suffered perfectly. None of us do. In my worst moments, I have been oblivious to how my responses harmed those around me. At this point in Psalm 73, Asaph has come to an awareness of how he acted when he was at his lowest point. He acted stupidly, like an unthinking animal. That is sobering.

- At times we have all been insensitive and self-absorbed in response to our own pain. And amid our own suffering, our indifference, impatience, or even hostility to others may have felt justified. But looking back, our careless words inflicted harm on others. How have you harmed others in your suffering?

I encourage you to be tender with yourself. There is no condemnation in Christ Jesus (Romans 8:1). Because he has paid for our sins, we can face any harm we have done to others, own it with them, and repair as we can. There is great freedom in Jesus to face our mistakes and sin head-on.

Despite Asaph's growing awareness of his own unthinking, self-absorbed actions when he was suffering, he doesn't dwell in self-condemnation: "Yet I am always with you; you hold me by my right hand" (v. 23). This image is comforting. God is the Father, holding his young child by the hand. Asaph may have been rude, even stupid, but God does not condemn him. Instead, God guides him by the hand through it: "You guide me with your counsel, and afterward you will take me up in glory" (v. 24). God's compassion and wisdom in spite of Asaph's shortcomings are in the spotlight here.

- Asaph models for us repentance that is distinct from worldly sorrow and self-condemnation. Worldly sorrow just leaves us feeling bad. Godly sorrow leads to repentance and repair with the one we have wronged (2 Corinthians 7:10). Have you felt worldly sorrow or godly sorrow over your sins and failures? What is the difference?

- Remember that Paul tells us in Romans 8:1, "There is now no condemnation for those who are in Christ Jesus." Instead of condemning Asaph, what four realities does Asaph experience after entering God's sanctuary according to verses 23 and 24?

To close today, is there anything you need to confess before God in your responses to God or others as you have suffered? Receive his gift of grace, and personalize the truths in verses 23 and 24 as a response to his grace and forgiveness.

Yet I am always with you; you hold my right hand. You guide me with your counsel, and afterward you will take me up in glory.

PSALM 73:23-24

PSALM 73:25-28 DAY 5

As we come to the end of Psalm 73, we find Asaph in a very different place from where we found him on days one and two of this week. In reality, nothing had changed in Asaph's circumstances, but everything had changed in his perspective. Asaph brought his demoralizing confusion and grief over the prosperity of the wicked to God, and in God's sanctuary Asaph found the grace and mercy he needed to look forward in hope.

Read today's passage three times slowly, asking God to speak to you through his Scriptures each time. Then, on your last reading, note the phrases that stand out to you.

Read Psalm 73:25-28.

- What phrases stood out to you in today's reading?

- Asaph started Psalm 73, "God is indeed good to Israel. . . . But as for me . . ." How had Asaph's understanding of both God and his circumstances changed by the end of the psalm?

Asaph says that though his own strength fails, God is his strength and his portion forever. "Portion" refers to an inheritance, usually a tract of land that would provide for the son or daughter who inherited it. I live on my grandparents' farm. It was initially 600 acres. After my grandfather's death, it was divided among his five children. Two sold their part. Another is building a house on his. My parents farmed their part, and now they and two of their children live on what remains. This land has been a source of income and stability for four generations of my family now. In Asaph's time, a portion of land given as an inheritance was similarly stabilizing.

Asaph felt destabilized by his circumstances. His foot had nearly slipped. But God was his portion, his stabilizing inheritance that provided for him when his own resources failed.

- Is your strength failing? Do you lack financial, spiritual, physical, or emotional resources? In what ways do you lack stabilizing resources?

- Asaph found in God the resources he needed to persevere in hope. How might God's eternal resources stabilize you in the midst of hard earthly circumstances?

God's presence was Asaph's good, and Asaph ends Psalm 73 holding God's hand, tucked safely into God's arms. God himself was Asaph's refuge. Asaph entered the physical temple, but he found God himself, not the temple walls, to be his true refuge.

As we end this week, close your eyes and imagine walking with a weary Asaph into the temple and taking in its stone palm trees and almond blossoms, its lampstands shaped in the likeness of the tree of life. Imagine the stone transforms from mere carvings to living greens and pinks. The walls fade, and you are in the presence of God himself. Imagine God gently wiping every tear from your face, leading you to the tree of life of Revelation 22 so that you can deeply rest in its shade. Imagine God holding you by the right hand as you wake up, infusing you with his strength and promising you his unfailing safety net in your life as you re-enter your earthly circumstances.

In closing, affirm these words of Asaph to God in prayer.

Yet I am always with you;
you hold my right hand.
You guide me with your counsel,
and afterward you will take me up in glory.
But as for me, God's presence is my good.
I have made the Lord God my refuge,
so I can tell about all you do.

WEEK FIVE | LISTEN TO MY PRAYER—PSALM 55

Group Session Introduction

This week, as we study Psalm 55, we are going to look at the pain of brokenness and alienation in our closest relationships in the church and home. To start us off, let's reflect on the story of Hagar from Genesis 16 and

21. God's interactions with her in the midst of her pain and alienation reflect and reinforce the message of Psalm 55. ***Watch this week's video.***

DISCUSSION

Read together Genesis 16:6-15 and Genesis 21:8-21. Remember, though our circumstances are different than Hagar's, our God is the same.

- How can abuse at the hands of those who claim to know and serve God affect our views of God and the Bible?
- What emotions and fears do you think Hagar felt when she was pregnant and first ran away from Sarai? What do you think she felt the second time when she and Ishmael had been pushed out and abandoned by Abraham?
- Notice that both times God found Hagar, not the other way around. What does this tell us about God's character and actions?
- In verse 16:11, God tells Hagar to name her son *Ishmael*, which in the Hebrew means "God hears." Why did God want her to name her son this?
- What is significant about Abram naming the boy Ishmael, considering that he was not there when God told Hagar to do so?
- In their first interaction, God made promises to Hagar about Ishmael's future, but Hagar's focus was on the Lord himself, not the promises. Why do you think she was more taken in by her interaction with God

himself than the promises he made to her about Ishmael?

- God told Hagar to return to Sarai and submit to her authority. This is hard. Why do you think Hagar was willing to return to this hard situation?

- Read Genesis 25:7-9. The chapter later tells of Ishmael's descendants who seemed numerous and stable. What are the implications of Ishmael returning to bury his father with Isaac?

Some traditions view Ishmael as an instigator of current conflicts with Israel. But that isn't based on evidence from the Scriptures. Islamic conflicts in Israel had their origins in the Middle Ages. Islam was founded in the 7th century AD in Saudi Arabia, thousands of years and miles removed from when and where Ishmael lived and died.

- As you think back on times you or your loved ones have felt unseen or unheard, what is the significance for you of these names for God, *El-Roi* (the God who Sees) and *Ishma-el* (the God who Hears)?

This week, as we study Psalm 55, we will focus on our God who sees and hears us. Remember from week two that God is compassionate. He is not distant from or oblivious to our hardships and sorrows. Be comforted this week that God sees you, hears you, and knows you. He has a plan for you that is certain and meaningful.

- Think of any experiences that have made you feel unseen. Perhaps you're caught in conflict with a family member or a colleague. Or maybe you've experienced some form of injustice—in your family, church, or community. Or maybe you feel misunderstood or taken for granted. How has your experience of feeling unseen affected you emotionally, physically, or spiritually?

Close in prayer asking God to open our eyes this week to the help both Hagar's story and Psalm 55 give us when we feel alienated or harmed by those who were supposed to be spiritually, physically, and emotionally safe for us.

PSALM 55:1-8 DAY 1

King David, author of Psalm 55, is a complicated figure in Scripture. He was both hunter and hunted, archer and prey. Like those hiding from dictators who would assassinate them, David fled for his life in caves as a young man. He'd been anointed by God to be king, but he had to rely on the good will of others to hide and feed him. Later, after he ascended to the throne, David was forced to flee for his life when his own son sought to kill him and take his throne. But David also preyed on others, taking from Uriah and Bathsheba what was not his to take, killing Uriah in the process.

David's legacy is complex, yet his groaning under the weight of humanity's fall rings honest to the suffering we all experience, whether we live in modern or ancient times. In Psalm 55, commentators think David was groaning under the weight of his betrayal by his son, Absalom, and his trusted advisor, Ahithophel. The language he used to describe betrayal will help us as we cry out to God amid our own suffering.

Ask God to open your eyes and give you supernatural help from the Scriptures for the suffering you experience personally or for suffering in the world at large. Then, read today's passage slowly three times. On your last reading, note words or phrases that stand out to you.

Read Psalm 55:1-8.

- What words or phrases resonated with you in today's reading?

- What does David ask of God in verses 1 and 2? What is implied by his request?

- Describe a time when you felt you had to beg God to hear your prayers. What circumstances caused you to feel that way?

- What are the circumstances surrounding David's experience of suffering (v. 3)?

- Why do you think David longed to fly away in response to his suffering? How do you identify with him?

David longed to be like a bird that could fly away, far removed from the conflict in his life. I, too, long at times to completely disengage from circumstances that vex me. Amusement becomes my coping mechanism and escape.

To *muse* means to think. *A-muse* means to not think. My suffering often leaves me looking for things that help me disengage and turn off my brain. While there is certainly a need at times for a reprieve from our circumstances, amusement can be an overused, unhealthy coping mechanism for me.

- How has amusement played a role in helping you disengage from hard circumstances? In what ways has it been helpful? In what ways has it been harmful?

Often, it has been the people for whom I am responsible, particularly my children, who have kept me engaged with real life. David was king, and he was responsible for the welfare of many; he could not simply disengage. He models for us what we need in such moments. Instead of disengaging from his circumstances, David reengaged with God.

- Have you had a time when you did not turn to God in prayer though you knew you needed to? What kept you from praying?

Stories are told of babies in some orphanages who stop crying because they learn that no one will come to their aid. Even after adoption, these children can have reactive attachment disorder and struggle to connect to anyone. They have lost (at least temporarily) the ability to trust that someone will help them. When our prayers seemingly go unanswered for long periods of time, we can experience a similar form of spiritual detachment. If God won't come to my aid, why keep asking? In these seasons, I fight the temptation to disengage altogether. This is a real struggle for many believers.

- Think of a time of spiritual detachment in your own life or the life of a loved one. What was the result in your or their life?

God, listen to my prayer
and do not hide from
my plea for help.
Pay attention to me
and answer me.
I am restless and in turmoil
with my complaint.

PSALM 55:1-2

In Psalm 55, David spurs us to reengage God on unanswered prayers and situations in which we cannot get away from our enemies. God preserved David's cry from long ago to assist us today when we grow weary of asking God for help. Do not stop turning to God. Implore God as David did.

Close today's study by praying verses 1 and 2, personalizing it for yourself or a loved one.

DAY 2 PSALM 55:1-16

I HAVE WITNESSED or been directly involved in four church conflicts. Three happened in my youth, and I mostly sat on the sidelines, pondering the disconnect between what I thought was supposed to hold Christians together and what I witnessed dividing the adults in my life. Another conflict happened in my adulthood, in a church where I actively served both with those who caused the harm and those who were harmed by spiritual abuse. That church had a vibrant ministry reaching young adults with no Christian background. It was deeply disturbing to watch friends turn on friends and the church eventually fall apart.

Church conflict and spiritual abuse are disorienting, because when they occur, the people who should be the safest for us are the ones causing the harm. David articulated his feelings of disorientation in Psalm 55. He experienced betrayal by those he counted as family and friends, those who were supposed to help him as God's anointed king. His lament can help us name the disorienting pain we feel when we are betrayed or misused by other Christians.

Following our usual method, ask God to open your eyes to his truth in this Scripture. Then read the passage slowly three times. Note words or phrases that stand out to you on the last reading.

READ PSALM 55:1-16.

- What words or phrases caught your attention?

- In verses 12-13, how does David describe his previous relationship with the one who now insults and betrays him?

David is vexed because this person who had been his peer, companion, and friend turned on him to the point that David feared for his own life. *Companion* (used in the CSB in verse 13) is an interesting word. Like *compassion*, it starts with the prefix *com*, meaning "together." *Panion* comes from the Latin for "bread." In the Latin, the word refers to someone with whom one breaks bread or shares a meal. It implies an intimate level of togetherness. We may work with cohorts, but we eat with friends. Theologians believe David is talking about his own counselor, Ahithophel. This friend and advisor plotted against David with his son Absalom. The level of betrayal by his close friend and his son tore at David's emotions.

- David struggled with the difference between betrayal by an enemy and betrayal by a close friend. How does betrayal by a friend complicate the harm and its aftermath in our lives?

- How does betrayal by Christian ministry leaders complicate our relationship with the church or other believers?

- Contrast verses 1-2 with verse 16. How has David's tone changed?

- As we close today's study, write out your prayer to God, personalizing verses 1, 2, and 16.

PSALM 55:16-23

DAY 3

How long should we lament to God? Is there a time limit for our lamentations? During week four, we studied Psalm 73. There Asaph started with bitter complaint, but after he entered God's sanctuary his perspective completely changed and his complaints ended. Not so with Psalm 55. David's complaints intermingle with his words of confidence in God throughout the psalm. This lament reflects little of the structure typical to David's poetry in the psalms; his back and forth between complaint *to* God and comfort *from* God is realistic, though. We also can lament and praise in the same breath.

David's struggle, which he cycles through again in today's section of the psalm, was caused by a close friend's treachery. The feelings that resulted from this betrayal were like a wasp David swatted away but that returned again and again to harass him. I have experienced similar feelings over one friend in particular, and I still struggle years later to put the situation to rest in my brain. When I think I am past their betrayal, something triggers the pain anew. I'm confounded, confused, and feel demoralized all over again when I remember the sweet times I experienced with this friend who now treats me as an enemy.

Following our normal method, ask God to open your eyes to his help and solidarity in the Scripture reading today. Then read the passage three times slowly. On your last reading, highlight words or phrases that stand out to you.

Read Psalm 55:16-23.

- What phrases did you note in today's Scripture? Why or how did they affect you?

Consider the language David uses to describe his betrayal. David's friend was "[violent] against those at peace with him." His words seemed buttery smooth, but all the while war was in his heart. Most importantly, David's friend broke covenant. *Covenant* is a loaded word in the Scriptures. It references a sober commitment, the faithfulness necessary for a relationship to reliably function. Truth is key to human flourishing, which is why God prohibited lying in the Ten Commandments.

- Has someone broken trust or abandoned their commitment to you? How did that harm your relationship with them? How did it affect your other relationships?

- What imagery did David use in verse 21 to describe his friend's betrayal?

- Interspersed with his complaints, David articulated his faith in God. What did David believe about God in verses 16-23 despite his friend's betrayal?

David ended this psalm with the words "But I will trust in you." In the previous verse, he reminded us to cast our burden on the Lord, who will sustain us and keep us upright. David used God's covenant name, Yahweh.

Though his friend had broken trust with David, God had not. God is a covenant-keeping God. Others may break faith, and others may lie. But God never will. He sustains us, and he will not allow us to be shaken off the sure and eternal foundation he provides.

As we end today's study, take time to pray that God would solidify your confidence in him when all others fail you.

GENESIS 16:7-16 — DAY 4

IN PSALM 55, David cycles through complaint and hope. Verses 17-18 sum up the psalm.

> I complain and groan morning, noon, and night,
> and he hears my voice.
> Though many are against me,
> he will redeem me from my battle unharmed.

In the opening video and discussion for this week, we reflected on the story of Hagar. She was a living example of what David would write in Psalm 55 hundreds of years after her life. God heard her voice, and she named her son Ishmael, which literally means "God hears." For the last two days of this week, we will review her story and meditate on the truth that God hears us and sees us. He hasn't left us alone to navigate betrayal by others.

Today's passage in Genesis occurs after Hagar, a slave bought in Egypt for Abram's wife Sarai, ran away from her abusive mistress after she became pregnant by Abram. Abram was God's chosen man—through his family, God would eventually send Jesus. But this story reveals ugly sin in the family that was supposed to become a beacon of God's grace to the nations.

Hagar's name meant to take flight or flee. It is an appropriate name for one who had no context where she was safe and could plant herself firmly. Instead, at multiple points in her life, both as a slave in Egypt and in Abram's household, she was uprooted at others' whims. Genesis 16 records how she fled from Abram and Sarai.

Read today's passage three times slowly. Between each reading, ask God to open your eyes to beautiful things in the Scriptures. Then note any words or phrases that stand out to you.

Read Genesis 16:7-16.

- What did you note about Hagar's situation and interaction with God?

The woman whose name meant "flight" had indeed fled. Even God's people used and abused her while she was in their care. Eventually, the law God would give to Abram's descendants would forbid and punish what Abram and Sarai did to Hagar, but at this point, there was no just resolution. Yet God found Hagar, not the other way around.

- What is the importance of "the angel of the Lord" finding Hagar?

- How does this fact help you when you feel unseen or unheard?

- The angel of the Lord told Hagar four things in verses 9-11. What were they?

- The first thing God told Hagar was hard—to return to her harsh mistress and submit to her authority (v. 9). How did Hagar respond to this instruction from God?

- Abram named his son Ishmael, indicating that Hagar told Abram about her experience with God, and Abraham believed her. Why do you suppose God wanted Hagar to name her son "God hears"?

- God made promises to Hagar that he made to no other woman in Scripture. Look up Genesis 15:3-6 and Genesis 26:23-25. Who else did God make such promises to?

Ishmael's name seems like a redemption of Hagar's name. Hagar lived a life of displacement and fled her harsh mistress. But amid her displacement, God found her, saw her, and heard her cries. The woman who fled became the woman God heard and established. She was both misused by humanity and kept safe by God.

- God told Hagar intriguing things about her son (v. 12), but that was not Hagar's focus as she responded to God. What was Hagar's focus during this encounter (v. 13)? How did she respond to God?

- What unjust situations are you, a loved one, or your community facing right now? Is there anything you are fleeing physically, emotionally, or spiritually? If you are in actual physical danger, please reach out to a friend, family member, or pastor for help.

As we close today, bring any unjust situation you or a loved one is facing to God in prayer and ask him to guide you to the help you or they need. Know that you pray to the God who hears and the God who sees.

HAVE YOU EVER BEEN SO DISTRESSED or discouraged that it did not even occur to you to bring your needs to God in prayer? I have. When the psychotic break of a loved one made me question my own reality. When the nurse let slip that my biopsy was cancerous. When I got the call that a family member had been murdered. Those situations left me stunned, and I was unable to grasp them or cope for a time. It is almost like I blacked out spiritually.

I wish it was only those shocking moments that caused spiritual blackout. But the reality is that anytime my immediate circumstances engulf 100 percent of my thoughts—whether it's a conflict with my children, an unexpected bill, or a dropped ball at work—I'm at risk of forgetting that I can bring anything and everything to God in prayer.

- Have you had a point of deep crisis when you did not go to God? Why didn't you go to him?

One of the goals of this eight-week study is to encourage you to bring your grief, pain, and questions directly to God. God promises his grace and mercy when we approach him in our time of need. Unlike us, Hagar didn't have the written Scriptures. She didn't have the Psalms or the book of Hebrews to encourage her to bring her troubles directly to God. Instead, God found her, not once but twice.

Fourteen or so years after Ishmael's birth, Hagar was again in a crisis not of her own making. As we end this week, let's reflect on concepts we first noted in this week's video and group discussion. Read through today's passage twice slowly, praying to God between each reading. Note words or phrases about Hagar's situation and God's response that stand out to you.

READ GENESIS 21:2-21.

- What did you notice about Hagar's response to her circumstances? How do you identify with her response?

Hagar had previously named her son Ishmael, "God hears," and called God *El-Roi*, "the God who Sees." But fourteen years later, that encounter seems far from her mind. Abraham sends Hagar and Ishmael away, and when their resources run out, Hagar physically distances herself from her son—she can't bear to see or hear his distress. But the God who sees and hears indeed sees and hears both her and Ishmael. Hagar may have forgotten their earlier encounter, but God has not forgotten her.

- Luke 19:10 says Jesus came to seek and to save the lost. Can you look back on a time in your life when God initiated with you, even though you were not seeking him yourself? What were the circumstances, and how did God engage you?

- What was God's assurance to Hagar for her son, Ishmael?

- For my mother's heart, Genesis 21:20 is one of the sweetest verses in all of Scripture. As a mom of two young men, the phrase "God was with the boy" sums up all I could hope for my children. How does the end of Hagar and Ishmael's story move your heart?

In Psalm 55, David cried out to God to hear him in his distress.

But I call to God,
and the LORD will save me.
I complain and groan morning, noon, and night,
and he hears my voice. (vv. 16-17)

Psalm 55 teaches us to cry out to God in persevering prayer. But the truth is that God pursues us relentlessly as well. *He seeks us out when we don't have the wherewithal to find him.* God found Hagar when she was lost—not once, but twice. He had a plan for her and Ishmael when she had no resources or direction.

- Why do you think God preserved in his Scriptures the story of Hagar as well as David's prayer in Psalm 55?

- The God who Sees and the God who Hears *sees and hears you*. With that confidence, write out your lament to God today. Remember that lament includes both complaint and hope. Include hope today in God's character as you reflect on God's pursuit of Hagar when others rejected her.

I complain and groan morning, noon, and night, and he hears my voice.

PSALM 55:17

WEEK SIX | I THINK OF YOU AND GROAN—PSALM 77

Group Session Introduction

Today we will talk about disillusionment and faith as we introduce Psalm 77. This psalm was written during a time in Israel's history when everything God had done for his people seemed to unravel. After a long season of the people choosing idols over God, Solomon's temple—which represented God's presence with his people—was destroyed. The righteous prophets warned the people of the consequences of their idolatry again and again, but they wouldn't listen. Imagine how frustrating and discouraging it was for those prophets.

To prepare to study Psalm 77 this week, we will look at one of the

prophets who lived and prophesied in this tumultuous season of disobedience that led to the destruction of the first temple.

Watch this week's video.

DISCUSSION

- In today's video, we heard Habakkuk's lament that the law seemed ineffective, and that even when it was applied, justice came out bent. In what ways have you seen Habakkuk's disillusionment play out in contemporary Christianity?
- How do people typically respond to churches or spiritual leaders who do harm instead of good or to Christian ministries that seem healthy but then fall apart?
- Read Ephesians 2:8-9. Why is *faith* such an essential word in Christianity?
- How have you heard others using the word *faith* or the phrase *Christian faith*? What do they typically mean by it?
- Read Hebrews 11:1-3. What unseen things are important to the Christian belief system?

- Read Hebrews 11:6. It clarifies what Scripture means when it uses the word *faith*. According to this passage, what two beliefs are essential to faith?
- We all experience doubt at different times. What situations make it hard to believe that God truly exists? What has helped when you have struggled with doubt?
- What makes it difficult to believe God is good to those who follow him? What helps?
- What good things have you been hoping for without visible proof they will happen? Name an underlying Christian hope you have not yet seen realized.
- Verse 6 speaks directly to the theme of this Bible study: *lament is a means of God's grace to us*. How do the truths that God exists and that he rewards those who seek him reinforce our theme?

Philippians 1:6 is a great verse to hold on to and pray through when we are longing for God to work in our homes, communities, and churches but things seem to be falling apart instead of growing stronger:

> I am sure of this, that he who started a good work in you will carry it on to completion until the day of Christ Jesus.

In closing, let's pray together that God would increase our confidence that he will do exactly what he says he will do, even when we don't yet see evidence of it.

PSALM 77:1-9

DAY 1

HAS GOD STOPPED MAKING SENSE TO YOU?

In the video for this week's study, I spoke about the confusion I experienced when my vibrant church, which brought many young people to Christ, completely fell apart due to the sin of its lead pastor. It wasn't that God had never done a good work in my life or community. The problem was that God had done a *great* work, a work that seemed to fit exactly what I thought he would want to do in my community. Then, it seemed to be utterly destroyed. If God is in control and loves his children, why did he allow sin to continue to the point that the church ended? I thought I understood what God was doing in my church and what he was doing in me. But afterward, I felt like I didn't understand anything at all.

What do we do when God stops making sense to us? Psalm 77 offers us help.

Psalm 77, like Psalm 73, which we studied in week four, is linked to Asaph. He was one of King David's chief musicians, but his name came to represent his descendants who were also musicians during and after the time of exile (Ezra 2:40-41).

Here the psalmist groans to God over the fall of Jerusalem and the destruction of Solomon's temple. In 586 BC, Nebuchadnezzar, king of Babylon, ransacked Jerusalem and destroyed Solomon's temple, which had stood for 400 years. This came after a long season of unrepentant idolatry among the kings and people of God. Many Jews, including Daniel and Jeremiah, were exiled to Babylon. The book of Esther tells of God's protection of his people in exile. After Babylon fell to Cyrus the Great, a remnant of the exiled Jews returned home and rebuilt the temple, as recounted in the books of Ezra and Nehemiah. The second temple was completed in 516 BC.

But at the writing of Psalm 77, God's temple was still in ruins, and his people were captive and exiled far from their homes. All the good God had done over thousands of years to give his children a land and a temple seemed to be undone in a generation. God stopped making sense to the psalmist. And the psalmist cried out to God in response.

With that context in mind, ask God to open your eyes to helpful truths in the Scriptures. Then read the passage three times slowly. On your last reading, note words or phrases that stand out to you.

Read Psalm 77:1-9

- What words or phrases did you note in today's reading?

- Verse 1 reminds us of what we discovered in week five in our study of Psalm 55 and God's comforting words to Hagar in the wilderness. In the context of church hurt and disillusionment, how does the promise that *God hears* affect you?

- In verses 2-4, the psalmist comes to God, but he doesn't find immediate release from his troubles. How does the psalmist experience God amid his groaning?

Verse 3 says, "I think of God; I groan; I meditate; my spirit becomes weak." This grabs my attention each time I read it. In week one, we defined suffering as our groaning under the weight of all that is wrong in the world since humanity's fall. Creation groans with us, and even God himself groans with us (Romans 8). But up to this point, we have not seen language about groaning caused by God himself. In Psalm 77, the psalmist thinks about *God* and groans. He meditates on God and becomes weaker, not stronger.

Psalms scholar Mark Futato says it this way, "Believing in a God who is not evidently at work in a time of deep trouble just adds insult to injury until we are virtually overwhelmed with longing for God to act on our behalf."

When my church in Seattle fell apart, it was painful to go to God in prayer over the situation. It was emotionally easier to distract myself than it was to be open and honest with God about the pain and disillusionment the situation caused in my heart.

- Consider a time when thinking about God seemed to make you feel worse, not better. Describe that situation and feeling.

- In verses 5-9, the psalmist contemplates past times in light of the present. What questions do these memories and meditations raise in his heart?

- Have you or a loved one asked questions similar to those in verses 7-9? What did or do you feel in terms of disillusionment with God?

- As we close today, name a situation in your life or a loved one's life when you have felt like God stopped working or has seemed to forget his promises. Psalm 77 models for us how to bring those very real situations and our questions to God. If you are thinking of a particular situation, bring it to God in prayer, and ask him the questions the situation has raised in your heart.

I cry aloud to God, aloud to God, and he will hear me.

PSALM 77:1

In the video for week two, we looked at the echoes of Eden that the Israelites would have encountered first in the tabernacle and then in Solomon's temple. God gave them these images to remind them that despite the losses at humanity's fall, God's character and plan had not changed. Solomon's temple was like a garden sanctuary made of masonry, gold, and jewels. It pointed back to the tree of life in Eden and forward to the one in Revelation, under whose shade we will sit for eternity with God.

This week's psalm laments the loss of that physical temple and those tangible reminders.

Psalm 77 is placed among the psalms of the exile. As the psalmist writes, Solomon's temple is in ruins, and the people have been taken far from the land meant to be their sanctuary. In Lamentations 2:7, Jeremiah describes it this way:

> The Lord has rejected his altar,
> repudiated his sanctuary;
> he has handed the walls of her palaces
> over to the enemy.

- When the temple was destroyed, it seemed like God was repudiating the temple and rejecting its entire point. At the time of this destruction, few of God's people worshiped and obeyed him. For generations, kings of Judah had built altars to false gods and refused to obey the one true God. But there was a remnant of faithful believers who still followed God and his law. How do you think the circumstances of Judah's captivity challenged men like Asaph and Jeremiah who still believed in the one true God?

- How would the destruction of God's temple have challenged you if you had lived through those times?

- Before we read today's passage, look back at your notes from week two, day two. Write out some of the unchanging attributes and purposes of God that we saw in Psalm 102.

Keep the reality of God's sovereignty and compassion in mind as you read today's passage. Following our normal method, read the passage through slowly three times, asking God to open your eyes to the beauty and help this Scripture provides. On your third reading, note any words or phrases that stand out to you.

READ PSALM 77:1-12.

- What words or phrases did you note as you read this Scripture passage?

- In these verses, we see both the psalmist's struggle and the beginning of his return to hope. What attributes of God does the psalmist question?

- Which of God's plans do you think the psalmist is doubting?

- In verses 7-9, the psalmist questions God's favor, his faithful love, his promise, his graciousness, and his compassion. Had God's character changed? Had he gotten so angry that he decided to stop showing compassion to the people he set apart hundreds of years before? What circumstances in your home, work, church, or community have caused you to similarly question God's character?

Asaph used the Hebrew word *hesed* in verse 8. God's faithful love, his hesed, is a theme throughout the Old Testament. In Exodus 34:6-7, God revealed his character and glory to Moses.

> The LORD passed in front of [Moses] and proclaimed:
>
> The LORD—the LORD is a compassionate and gracious God, slow to anger and abounding in faithful love and truth, maintaining faithful love [hesed] to a thousand generations, forgiving iniquity, rebellion, and sin. But he will not leave the guilty unpunished, bringing the consequences of the fathers' iniquity on the children and grandchildren to the third and fourth generation.

- In Exodus 34, what did God reveal about himself to Moses?

- In Psalm 77:10, Asaph grieved that God seemed to have forgotten his *hesed*, his faithful love for his children. Look at verses 11-12. What did Asaph do in response?

In closing today, let's remember God's faithful love in our own lives, communities, and churches. Pray today through verses 11 and 12.

I will remember the LORD's works;
yes, I will remember your ancient wonders.
I will reflect on all you have done
and meditate on your actions.

- As you pray, ask God to help you remember times his compassion and faithful love were clearly seen in your life. As situations come to mind, note them here.

PSALM 77:9-15 — DAY 3

FIRST SAMUEL 7 TELLS HOW the prophet Samuel erected a stone to help the Israelites remember a battle God won for them when they were too scared to defend themselves. That stone was called an *ebenezer*, which means "stone of help." In week five, we studied Hagar and Ishmael. Just as Ishmael's name would help Hagar remember her interaction with God in the wilderness, Samuel's stone would help the Israelites remember God's past faithfulness to them.

When I moved back to my parents' farm, I hoped to remodel my grandmother's farmhouse. Built in the 1930s, it sits in the shade of a giant live oak that reminds me of the tree of life. When I moved home, the old house still had its original windows. The interior walls were filled with snakeskins and chicken bones the mice had left over eight decades. And the electric wiring had only been replaced once, forty years before.

As a newly divorced mom without a job, I couldn't get approved for a loan to remodel the house. When I finally received the funds I needed to make the house livable, I knew God had provided in a way that I couldn't on my own. After my boys and I moved in, I had a stone marker engraved with 1

Samuel 7:12—our ebenezer—that we placed at the foot of the home's front porch steps.

When new trials came, like my cancer diagnosis the next year, the memory of God's provision of our home was a great help to me. Remembering how God had provided before, helped me to believe he would take care of my family again.

In today's section of Psalm 77, *the psalmist remembered*. And it helped him greatly.

Using our typical method, read today's passage three times slowly, asking God to open your eyes to helpful truths in the Scriptures. Then, on the last reading, note any words or phrases that stand out to you.

Read Psalm 77:9-15.

- What words or phrases stood out to you today?

- What grieved the psalmist in this section?

- In response to his grief, the psalmist wrote three "I will" statements. What were they?

Let's look at both the action the psalmist takes and the object of those actions. He will remember, reflect, and meditate. What is similar about those three words? What is different?

- The objects of these meditations and reflections are *the Lord's work, his ancient wonders, all he has done,* and *his actions*. What ancient wonders and actions had God done for Israel in the past? If you want some reminders, read Joshua 6, Exodus 14, or Exodus 16.

- Why would those past events in Israel's history be helpful for the psalmist to remember and meditate on?

- Many of the events the psalmist remembered had happened long before he was born. He wasn't meditating on God's work that he had witnessed personally, but the stories of God's faithfulness passed down from generations before him. What stories of God's faithfulness do you know from previous generations or from others in your church or community?

- What is the psalmist's response in verses 13-15 after meditating on God's past provisions?

The word *holy* is another often used, rarely defined, word in Christian circles. When the Bible uses the word, it means to be "set apart." Holy vessels in the temple were ones that were set apart for God's purposes and use. They may have looked similar to common bowls or pitchers an average Israelite would have used in their homes, but they were holy, set apart to be used only while worshiping God.

I will reflect on all
you have done
and meditate on your actions.
God, your way is holy.
What god is great like God?
You are the God who
works wonders;
you revealed your strength
among the peoples.
With power you redeemed
your people,
the descendants of Jacob
and Joseph. Selah

PSALM 77:12-15

God's ways, which the psalmist did not understand after the destruction of Solomon's temple, were nevertheless holy. God's ways were set apart for God's purposes. God started his plan in the Garden of Eden, in the shade of the tree of life. And despite humanity's sin, that is where we will end as well. God's ways are set apart for the movement of God's people toward that end.

God, your way is holy.

As we close in prayer today, I encourage you to make the psalmist's response to God from verses 12-15 your own.

PSALM 77:11-20

DAY 4

WHEN I WAS DIAGNOSED with cancer, I fell into a dark hole emotionally. I was still deep in the weeds of the mental health issues that had brought about my divorce, and this trial on top of the other one was too much to process, let alone endure.

In the weeks that led up to surgery, I walked the dirt loop around my farmhouse again and again in an effort to work through my antsy anxiety. On each lap, I would turn to see the front porch of my farmhouse, the one with 1 Samuel 7:12 engraved on a stone at its steps. It reminded me of another time when my back was against a wall. I felt trapped, and I couldn't figure out my own path forward. But, as Travis Greene sings, God made a way.

The author of Psalm 77 found comfort as he too remembered a time when Israel's back was against a wall, and they had no route of escape. Read today's passage three times slowly. Pray between each reading that God would speak to you through the Scriptures. On your last reading, note any words or phrases the Spirit has impressed on your heart.

READ PSALM 77:11-20.

- What words or phrases stood out to you? Why?

The psalmist focuses on the quintessential example of deliverance in Israel's history, the parting of the Red Sea after Moses led them away from slavery in Egypt. The Israelites had been slaves in Egypt for four hundred years. Finally, after a series of plagues, Pharaoh let the Israelites go (Exodus 7–12). But as they escaped, Pharaoh and his army pursued them, trapping them against the sea. In distress and fear, the Israelites turned on Moses. In Exodus 14:13-14 (NIV), Moses answers the people.

> Do not be afraid. Stand firm and you will see the deliverance the LORD will bring you today. The Egyptians you see today you will never see again. The LORD will fight for you; you need only to be still.

- What were Moses' instructions to the Israelites when their backs were against a wall and they could not make a way of escape for themselves?

God parted the sea for the Israelites to escape, and they were finally free of their slave masters. The memory of this supernatural deliverance became crucial for surviving the exile that was the context of Psalm 77. Once again Israel waited on God to free them from their foreign captors.

- Think of a time when you or a loved one had your back against a wall and couldn't make your own way of escape. How did the situation finally resolve?

In verse 19, the psalmist says

> Your way went through the sea
> and your path through the vast water,
> but your footprints were unseen.

- Take some time to meditate on this verse, and journal your reflections.

As we close today, ask God to open your eyes to the places where he has been and continues to be at work in your life, making a way forward for you and your loved ones even when you don't see his footprints.

PSALM 77:19-20

DAY 5

In this week's video, I told about my church in Seattle that in two years went from ten thousand attendees to completely disbanding after the lead pastor's unethical practices were made public. The decade that followed that church's failure was disorienting for me on multiple fronts. But today, fifteen years later, I am at peace in a small church plant in my hometown. The church has kind, humble leadership—the opposite of what I experienced in that Seattle megachurch.

Not everyone from my former church has had my experience, but in retrospect, I can see God's care and kindness to my family and many others through those disorienting circumstances. In the end, that church wasn't destroyed; it was dispersed, and many smaller congregations throughout that region and the world have benefitted from that dispersion, including my own little congregation in South Carolina.

One great thing about reading Scripture long after it was written is that we can look back and see how things played out for God's children over time. Psalm 77 is included in Book 3 of the Psalms. As we heard in this week's video, these psalms were likely first written and read when the Israelites were captive in Babylon. The book of Esther tells of God's sovereign care and protection of his people during this captivity when one of their foreign captors conspired to annihilate the Jewish people as a race. The books of Ezra and Nehemiah tell us how God worked in the heart of the foreign king Cyrus to allow the captives to return home and rebuild the temple. As in Egypt, God cleared the way before them, even if his footprints remained unseen. This second deliverance from a foreign captor was different from their first deliverance from Egypt through the Red Sea. But it was deliverance!

Read today's passage three times slowly. Ask God to open your eyes to see something in these verses you may not have seen up to this point.

Read Psalm 77:19-20.

- Verse 20 describes God's leadership using the language of sheep herding. This is language found throughout the Scriptures. Why do you think God uses the metaphor of shepherds and sheep so often in Scripture? What does this metaphor communicate to you?

- The most famous passage on shepherds and sheep is Psalm 23. Take a moment to read it now. What does the Good Shepherd do for the psalmist in the presence of his enemies?

- What do you think this shepherding language in Psalm 77 communicated to the Israelites when they were held in captivity in Babylon?

- How does this shepherding language help you when you think about the hard situations you face today?

As we close this week's meditations on Psalm 77, think about the ways God leads us like a flock of sheep. Pray through Psalm 23, claiming its description of the Good Shepherd's care for his sheep for yourself.

WEEK SEVEN | SAVE ME, GOD— PSALM 69

Group Session Introduction

This week, we are studying another psalm of David, Psalm 69. We have mentioned David's complicated presence in the Scriptures before. He was predator and prey, sinner and saint. He sinned terribly, but he also confessed his sin and turned back to God. His honesty about his emotions in

the wake of his own failures before God and sins against him make Psalm 69 a helpful psalm for us to examine this week. ***Watch this week's video.***

DISCUSSION

Today, we will read two different but overlapping passages that use the language of a "time of favor." Isaiah the prophet lived among idolatrous kings who aligned with bad rulers of neighboring lands, resulting in the northern tribes of Israel being absorbed into the pagan nations around them.

The northern tribes of Israel were conquered by Assyria around 722 BC and absorbed into neighboring lands. The southern tribes of Judah remained in the land until the fall of Jerusalem in 586 BC.

In this context, the prophet Isaiah received this prophecy of the coming Messiah.

The Spirit of the Lord God is on me,
because the Lord has anointed me
to bring good news to the poor.
He has sent me to heal the brokenhearted,
to proclaim liberty to the captives
and freedom to the prisoners;
to proclaim the year of the Lord's favor,
and the day of our God's vengeance;
to comfort all who mourn,

to provide for those who mourn in Zion;
to give them a crown of beauty instead of ashes,
festive oil instead of mourning,
and splendid clothes instead of despair. (Isaiah 61:1-3)

Discuss these questions about the passage.

- There are several contrasts in this passage. Considering the context in which it was written, in what ways were Isaiah's original audience captive, prisoners, brokenhearted, mourners, and despairing?
- What is the contrasting promise offered to each of those groups?

The second passage we read today is one we have read before (during week two). It is from Luke 4 when Jesus reads from Isaiah 61 in the synagogue.

[Jesus] came to Nazareth, where he had been brought up. As usual, he entered the synagogue on the Sabbath day and stood up to read. The scroll of the prophet Isaiah was given to him, and unrolling the scroll, he found the place where it was written:

The Spirit of the Lord is on me,
because he has anointed me
to preach good news to the poor.
He has sent me
to proclaim release to the captives
and recovery of sight to the blind,
to set free the oppressed,
to proclaim the year of the Lord's favor.

He then rolled up the scroll, gave it back to the attendant, and sat down. And the eyes of everyone in the synagogue were fixed on him. He began by saying to them, "Today as you listen, this Scripture has been fulfilled." (Luke 4:16-21)

Discuss the following questions about this second passage.

- What was your reaction to reading the final sentence in this passage?
- What views do you think Jesus' audience had of Isaiah 61 before his final words?

- How did Jesus proclaim release to captives?
- How did Jesus give sight to the blind literally and figuratively?
- In what ways does Jesus still set the oppressed free?
- How would you describe in your own words what "a time of favor" or "the year of the Lord's favor" means?
- What are the implications of Jesus' words in Luke 4 for you or your loved ones today?

This week, David gives us language in Psalm 69 that, once again, helps us articulate our pain and discouragement to God. But this psalm will also point to the eternal hope we have in Jesus. In him, we can have complete confidence that we are eternally secure in God's favor. One day, he will wipe away every tear as we sit eternally with him in the shade of the tree of life.

In closing, ask God to use Psalm 69 to help each of us bring our suffering to God this week, and pray God would help us believe that his favor is truly on us through Jesus.

In Psalm 69, David groans under the emotional, physical, and spiritual weights of a long season of distress. We don't know the exact circumstances that led to his writing this psalm, but his language is raw as he cries out to God for deliverance and help.

Using our usual method, read today's passage three times slowly. Between each reading, ask God to open your eyes to the ways this psalm helps you name and bring your own suffering to God. On your last reading, note words or phrases that stand out to you.

Read Psalm 69:1-4.

- What words or phrases did you note? How do you relate to them?

- David was skilled at using imagery to communicate his anguish. Consider each of the images he uses. What does each image communicate to you?

  The water has risen to my neck.

  I have sunk in deep mud, and there is no footing.

  I have come into deep water, and a flood sweeps over me.

The word *overwhelmed* comes to my mind when I read David's description of his emotional state amid his circumstances. *Whelm* is an Old English word for covering. A "whelming flood" would be a flood that covers houses, streets, and farmland. The rising waters of the 2011 tsunami in Japan were a whelming flood. Instead of massive white-capped waves, a steady influx of water grew and grew until it reached the first story of buildings, then the second, then the third, finally sweeping them away in their entirety.

Psalm scholar Mark Futato calls Psalm 69 a "psalm of disorientation." And a rising flood is disorienting. The waters rush into your safe hold, flush you out, and toss you among the flotsam and jetsam strewn in the water. Roofs become walls. Doors become windows. What once was a solid structure now floats in the current.

David was completely disoriented, overwhelmed by his circumstances and unable to find footing to get out of it.

- When have you or a loved one felt unable to get a foothold in the middle of a crisis? What were your internal and external responses?

In verse 3, David said he was worn out from crying, his throat was parched. He had run out of tears, not because his circumstances changed, but because he was dehydrated. His eyes failed as he looked for God. Many times, tears release endorphins, and a good cry can actually help us feel better—but David didn't feel better after crying. He felt worse.

- What thoughts or emotions does David's language in verse 3 evoke in you?

Verse 4 gives us insight into the particular circumstances that overwhelmed David. He was experiencing an intense interpersonal conflict that resulted in relational distress. David felt hated and deceived. People in his life wanted to destroy him, and David was left to pay the consequences of other's sin.

Though I did not steal, I must repay.

- How have you been left to clean up a mess you did not make?

We don't know what circumstances in David's life provoked this particular psalm. But it reminds me of the stress and anxiety in his life when he was anointed by Samuel to be the next king of Israel. At the time, there already was a king—Saul—and he hunted David relentlessly to kill him, blaming David for circumstances in his life that God, not David, had set in motion.

- David was caught in a storm he didn't create, repaying a debt he did not owe. I have often felt like a kite in someone else's hurricane. At times, I have felt like a kite in God's hurricane. Describe the frustrations of feeling like a kite in someone else's hurricane, tossed around by a storm you did not create.

- As we close, make David's prayer your own today: David cried, "Save me, God." Personalize his words in verses 1-4 today in prayer. God already knows your circumstances, but it helps us to bring them to his throne room, using the language he has given us in his Word when we don't have the words ourselves.

DAY 2 PSALM 69:5-12

David was both sinner and sinned against. He recognized that he could not put all the blame on others for the chaos that overwhelmed him. In the next portion of Psalm 69, David is honest before God about his own foolishness and guilt. His words prompt us to be honest about ours as well.

Read through today's passage three times slowly. Between each reading, ask God to open your eyes to any unconfessed sin you have committed against him or others.

Read Psalm 69:5-12.

- Did God bring to mind sin or foolishness that you need to confess? Remember that Jesus bore on the cross all the shame we might feel so we can be utterly freed from it. When we confess our sins, God is faithful and kind, and he forgives us (1 John 1:9). There is no condemnation for us in Christ Jesus (Romans 8:1). Write out your confession here.

David was concerned that his actions had harmed the nation's testimony about God, but he also expressed that his own genuine love for God had been mocked. The book of 2 Samuel tells one such story: before Saul was king, the Ark of the Covenant—the symbol of God's presence with his people—had been captured by their enemies, the Philistines. After David became king, one of his first acts was to get the ark and move it to Jerusalem where it would eventually sit in the temple built by his son Solomon. We read about David's joy as the ark came into the city in 2 Samuel 6:14.

> David was dancing with all his might before the LORD wearing a linen ephod.

The passage goes on to say that David's wife, Saul's daughter Michal, looked at him and despised him. David returned to his house in joy, but Michal mocked him and called him vulgar.

David lost himself in the joy of the occasion, and his own wife despised him for it. I have felt despised for my love of God at times. But I have also been the one despising others because their display of love for God didn't fit what I thought was appropriate.

- Has your faith in God resulted in others tearing you down? Or has another's strong love of God caused you to be the one who is embarrassed by them? In what way do you identify with this story of David and Michal?

In his Gospel, John quotes Psalm 69:9 as he describes Jesus turning over tables in the temple.

> His disciples remembered that it is written: "Zeal for your house will consume me." (John 2:17 NIV)

Jesus was angry at the ways the religious leaders had made the temple into a business instead of a place of worship. He too was despised during his life on earth for his zeal for God the Father. This is the first moment in Psalm 69 in which we start to see hints of Jesus, but it will not be the last.

- Today's reading from Psalm 69 covered a lot of ground. David sinning. David sinned against. David harming the testimony of God among the people. David mocked for his own exuberant love of God. What aspect of today's passage hits closest to home in your own life?

As you close in prayer, pray in gratitude that you sit in God's time of *eternal* favor on you. Ask him to open your eyes to what this means as you struggle with your own sin and testimony before God in your suffering.

TODAY, WE WILL STUDY DAVID'S CRY to God for "a time of favor." If you haven't yet watched the video that accompanies this week where I explore this language in depth, would you do so now?

- Do you long for a "time of favor"? I do. I long for a season when God would bless me in the ways I have seen him bless those around me. In your own words, describe the sort of life you would characterize as "favored."

Using our usual method, read today's passage three times slowly. At each reading, ask God to open your eyes to his help for the losses and longings you face today. On your third reading, note any words or phrases that stand out to you.

READ PSALM 69:13-18.

As he did in earlier verses, David again paints the picture of a whelming flood beneath which he can find no footing. For a long time in my own life, I felt like I was walking upstream against a rising current. Life's river rushed against me. It didn't always feel like the water would go over my head and sweep me away. But even when it didn't, I still felt mired down in the mud and held back by the current against me. My physical health remains an ongoing struggle. I have a form of juvenile arthritis that makes the transition from bed to standing, or from a chair to standing, very painful. My body consistently works against me as I try to get up and accomplish the tasks I need to do on any given day.

You might also have physical challenges. Or maybe there are relational challenges that feel like a current rushing against you, slowing you down. Whatever the challenge, it can cause both emotional and spiritual exhaustion.

- What circumstances in your life feel like rushing waters and miry clay working against your faith?

In the portion of Scripture we read today, David interspersed his cry for rescue with an appeal to God's faithful love and an affirmation of God's compassion. We explored God's *compassion* in week two. Our Savior is not dispassionate. He is not unaffected by the suffering we face or the weights we endure.

- Last week we briefly looked at the Hebrew word *hesed* which is translated frequently as "faithful love." It is the special name for God's covenant love, for his faithful commitment to his promises to his children. In addition to "faithful love," we see *hesed* also translated as "loving kindness," which tells us that this single Hebrew word is packed with meaning. It's *more* than kindness. It's more than faithfulness. It's more than love. How do the two words *faithful love* or *loving kindness*, when used together, help you understand the character of God?

God preserved Psalm 69 for all his children who struggle to endure circumstances that seem to work against them. David cried out for rescue, and he repeatedly begged God to answer him. The invitation is for you to do the same. Boldly come before God in your weariness. Remind God of his *compassion* and *faithful love*. Remind yourself too.

- Close today by making David's prayer in this section your own once again.

As we read further into Psalm 69 today, you may recognize language associated with Jesus' suffering and death in the New Testament. In the Old Testament, Christ is seen in David's zeal for God's house; he is seen in his sufferings too. In his *Classic Commentaries*, Derek Kidner notes the difference in the two—David cursed his tormentors while Jesus prayed for his.

Using our usual method, read today's verses three times slowly, praying to God for wisdom and insight between each reading. On your last reading, note words or phrases that stand out to you.

READ PSALM 69:19-28.

- What words or phrases did you note? Why did they resonate with you?

- Verses 19 and 20 have dual meaning. They reflect David's experience, but they also reflect Jesus' experience. David uses the words *insults*, *shame*, *disgrace*, and *despair*. How do these words reflect Jesus' experience on earth?

Jesus himself quoted Psalm 69 in John 15 as he prepared his disciples for his suffering on the cross.

> But this happened so that the statement written in their law might be fulfilled: "They hated me for no reason." (John 15:25)

The apostle Paul also quoted Psalm 69 in Romans as he encouraged the Roman church to put Christlike humility into practice.

> For even Christ did not please himself but, as it is written: "The insults of those who insult you have fallen on me." (Romans 15:3 NIV)

- In what ways can Jesus' endurance of unjust accusations, hate, and insults help you in the unjust situations you, your loved ones, or your community face today?

- Psalm 69:21 clearly reflects Jesus' crucifixion. Matthew 27:34 says that during the crucifixion, "they gave [Jesus] wine mixed with gall to drink. But when he tasted it, he refused to drink it." Jesus was thirsty, but soldiers gave him something that would only make his thirst worse, not better. Though it happened literally in Jesus' suffering, David likely referred to "gall" and "vinegar" as a metaphor for his sufferings. In what ways have you experienced responses to your suffering or need that worsened the pain instead of lessening it?

- In verses 22-28, David prayed for God to punish his enemies. Look up Matthew 5:43-45, a section of the Sermon on the Mount. Contrast David's prayer for vengeance with Jesus' teaching.

- What has been your response to those who insult, shame, or provoke despair in you, your loved ones, or your community?

As we close today, bring God both your hurt and your responses to others who have harmed you. Ask God to move you from David's perspective on his enemies to Jesus' perspective. This is a supernatural work that we cannot do by ourselves.

In week three, we worked through Psalm 88. There the psalmist lamented his deep pain before God. Notably, that psalm never moved to expressing hope or praising God. Not so with Psalm 69.

Using our regular method, read today's passage three times slowly. Between each reading, ask God to move you to praise and hope just as he moved David. On your last reading, note any words or phrases that stand out to you.

Read Psalm 69:29-36.

- What words or phrases did you note?

- According to verse 29, what was David's current state as he prayed to God?

- David prayed that God's salvation would protect him. Reflect on that language. What do you think David was really asking for himself?

From verse 30 to the end of the chapter, we see a phenomenon we have seen before in our journey through various psalms of lament. Though the psalmist's circumstances hadn't yet changed, his outlook had.

- What is your response to David's "I will praise" statement in verse 30?

- In Psalm 69:3, David said, "I am weary from my crying; my throat is parched. My eyes fail, looking for my God." Contrast that with verses 32-36. How has David's outlook changed?

- What is David confident God will do, according to the last verses of Psalm 69? How do these things apply to you today?

David began his lament in Psalm 69 in a very dark place. He cried until he had no more tears, unable to find God amid his suffering. But as his lament progressed, it began to reflect the way Christ would later suffer in David's place. God did a supernatural work in David's heart as he wrote and prayed. By the end of the psalm, though David's circumstances hadn't changed, his outlook had.

God listens to the cries of those who need him. He does not despise you or me when we are weak. God did not despise David's prayers in his weakness but met him in his weakness and helped him through it. Lament was a means of God's grace to David. *And it is to us as well.*

- What does it mean to you that God does not despise your lament?

As we close this week, I encourage you to pray this last section, personalizing it for yourself. Thank God that he does not despise your prayers. Thank him that he listens and he promises grace and mercy in your time of need. Ask for that grace and mercy for the specific circumstances and people you are struggling with right now.

WEEK EIGHT | RESTORE OUR FORTUNES, LORD—PSALM 126

Group Session Introduction

For the final week of our study, we will work through Psalm 126. Though it speaks of weeping, it is not technically a psalm of lament. It falls in Book 5 of the Psalms and is called a psalm of ascent. Commentators think these psalms were ones that were sung by the exiles on their return journey to Jerusalem or as they ascended the steps to the rebuilt temple after their return.

Watch this week's video.

DISCUSSION

Psalm 126 pictures believers sowing in tears while also anticipating reaping a harvest with joy. The big point is this: We do not need to be past weeping or grieving to sow for the future.

Read Psalm 126 aloud together.

When the Lord restored the fortunes of Zion,
we were like those who dream.
Our mouths were filled with laughter then,
and our tongues with shouts of joy.
Then they said among the nations,
"The Lord has done great things for them."
The Lord had done great things for us;
we were joyful.

Restore our fortunes, Lord,
like watercourses in the Negev.
Those who sow in tears
will reap with shouts of joy.
Though one goes along weeping,

carrying the bag of seed,
he will surely come back with shouts of joy,
carrying his sheaves.

For our discussion today, we are going to focus on the language of verse 6. It starts, "Though one goes along weeping." This psalm of ascent on sowing and reaping does not indicate that God's people had to wait until they were done grieving losses to begin sowing for the future. God's people could do both.

- The Bible uses farming metaphors throughout Scripture to illustrate God's work in the world. What are some pastoral and agricultural metaphors in the Bible that help us to picture life and loss? (Consider Psalm 23; 1 Corinthians 15:42-43; Matthew 13; John 12:24; Luke 20; or James 5:7.)
- What does the bag of seed (v. 6) represent in the metaphor of sowing while weeping?
- What problems and stresses do you imagine the Israelites faced when they returned to their devastated homes after the exile? Nehemiah 1:3 gives a general idea.
- Why is sowing with weeping an apt metaphor for the Israelites' situation as they returned to their homeland?
- Verse 6 is written for those who are still weeping. Perhaps the initial shock of the circumstances that caused our suffering has worn off, but we continue to grieve because our losses are permanent. What losses have you, your loved ones, or your community experienced that fit this category?
- Where are you in your own process of lament?
- What bags of seed has God given specifically to you, your church, or your community?
- What barriers have kept you from feeling equipped to move forward in sowing the seed God has put at your feet?
- How can you encourage others who are mourning to continue sowing?

Psalm 126 encourages us that lamenting does not have to keep us from simultaneously reengaging with the work Christ has for us. Our losses might bring limitations, but with those losses, God provides new and different seed for us to sow in his kingdom. As we end our time together, let us pray with thankfulness that God hears us when we cry out to him, welcomes our words of grief and suffering, and still has good work for us to do in his name.

CLOSING PRAYER

Thank you God that you assure us of your grace and mercy when we come to you at our lowest points and greatest need. We know one day we will be free from mourning and grief, sitting in the shade of the tree of life as you gently wipe the tears from our face. Until that day, we pray for open eyes to see the bags of seed you have placed at our feet, and for courage to sow this seed for your kingdom. Even though our eyes, for now, are still wet with tears, your promise is joy—a joy that is hard for us to imagine now. Guide us as we grieve. Bless us as we sow. We look to you to bring a harvest we cannot imagine ourselves.

PSALM 126:1-3 — DAY 1

Psalm 126 is a psalm of ascent. In the video, we discussed that these psalms were likely recited by God's people as they returned to Jerusalem from exile or journeyed to the temple for the yearly feasts and festivals. In this week's video, we focused on the last three verses of the psalm. In today's study, let's focus on the first three.

Using our usual method, read the verses slowly three times. Between each reading, ask God to open your eyes to his message for you in these verses. On your last reading, note words or phrases that stand out to you.

Read Psalm 126:1-3.

- What did you note about these verses as you read them? Why did that stand out to you?

- Did you notice that these verses are all in the past tense? Write out the past-tense verbs from the passage.

- These first three verses recite the people's memories. Whatever losses they were experiencing in the present, this song recalled God's help and provision in the past. Why is it hard to remember God's blessing and provision in the past when we are hurting in the present?

In our study of Psalm 77 in week six, we talked about remembering God's past faithfulness. I told you about the rock I had engraved with 1 Samuel 7:12, where Samuel "took a stone and set it upright between Mizpah and Shen. He named it Ebenezer, explaining, 'The Lord has helped us to this point.'" Like the stone Samuel set up, my little stone has helped me to remember God's faithfulness to provide for my family when I could not do it myself.

In Psalm 126, the children of Israel remember.

- What did they remember?

- When you look back at your life and the life of your church and community, how has God provided in the past?

- Do you have any markers that help you remember God's past provision? I have the engraved stone by my porch steps. I also have two Scripture promises I read during the days leading up to my divorce that I made into wall hangings to remind me of God's care for me. Some Christians hang pictures of events from the Scriptures, perhaps the parting of the Red Sea or manna on the ground in the wilderness as reminders of God's past faithfulness. If you don't have any visual reminders of God's faithfulness around you, what is one you could add around your home or office? It doesn't have to be Scripture; it could be a photograph or memento that reminds you of a season of your life.

- What lessons about God can you gather from how he provided in the past for you, your community, or his children in the Bible?

As we close today's study, allow memories of God's past faithfulness to help you as you call out to him over new situations that seem to have no resolution. Ask God to help you remember his past provision. Ask him to open your eyes to what his past provision teaches about his character and how it helps you in the current struggles you face.

YESTERDAY, WE FOCUSED on the first three verses of Psalm 126. We saw that remembering God's help in the past is an aid for us in the present to sow new seed despite ongoing grief. Today, we will read through the entire chapter and think about the transition from past provision to current struggle.

Using our usual method, read the psalm three times slowly. Between each reading, ask God to open your eyes to important truths from this psalm for you today. On your last reading, note words or phrases that stand out to you, perhaps something you have not noted before.

Read Psalm 126.

- What, if anything, new stood out to you in today's reading?

Did you notice the transition from verse 3 to verse 4? God had done great things for his children. The implication is that it didn't seem like he was doing great things for them at the current time. They asked God to "restore their fortunes" like "watercourses in the Negev."

The Negev is a desert region in southern Israel. The "watercourses" spoken about in Psalm 126 were the dry river beds in the region that only filled after rains. The metaphor in verse 4 is clear. The people experienced seasonal drought literally. But like us, they also experienced figurative drought—a drought of hope and faith.

- How does the word drought apply to experiences of suffering you have faced?

Whatever type of drought God's children faced in Psalm 126, it was fundamentally a drought of resources. Their prayer makes this clear. "Restore our fortunes," they cried. While remembering God's past provision is helpful, even necessary to persevere in hard seasons, a turn of fortune and loss of resources after past blessing can be particularly painful.

- Think of a time that you, or someone in your community, had a turn of fortune—a time when you enjoyed God's blessing only to see it snatched away. Describe the circumstances. What were the physical, emotional, or spiritual resources that seemed lost as a result?

When God's children asked him to restore their fortunes, they addressed him as LORD. The word Lord when spelled in all capitals refers to God's proper name, "Yahweh." This is the name God revealed to Moses in Exodus 3. It's related to the Hebrew phrase God spoke when he declared his existence to Moses at the burning bush: "I am who I am."

In week six, we discussed Hebrews 11, which teaches that belief in God's existence is core to what it means to have faith.

> Now without faith it is impossible to please God, since the one who draws near to him must believe that he exists and that he rewards those who seek him. (Hebrews 11:6)

When Israel was exiled from the land, it was clear they'd had a change in fortune. But while the nation's circumstances had changed, their God had not. He still existed, and he existed with the same good character he always had. His existence was an anchor they held onto despite their temporal circumstances.

- How can the truth of God's existence, despite your circumstances, anchor you when your fortunes change and your resources feel depleted?

Hebrews 11 says that God rewards those who seek him. In Psalm 126, God's people were still seeking him, despite the change in their fortunes. That is what we have been doing for the last seven weeks as well. Day after day, we have been turning back to God despite the hard circumstances many of us face. We have been seeking his help through it all.

God is good to those who seek him.

Restore our fortunes, LORD, like watercourses in the Negev.

PSALM 126:4

As we close, turn once again to God in prayer. Personalize verse 4 in prayer to God for yourself, your loved ones, or your community. Name the loss, and ask for restoration.

DAY 3 PSALM 126:4-6

When my divorce became final, circumstances forced me to leave my home, church, and community in Seattle, Washington, the only neighborhood my children had ever known. By the time I moved to my grandparents' farm in South Carolina, I was gutted and barely functioning. But the slow rhythms of the farm began to comfort me long before I understood what was happening. Plowing fields, sowing seeds, watering plants, removing weeds, and harvesting crops. Again and again.

The farming cycle is a metaphor for life.

Using our usual method, read today's passage three times slowly. Between each reading, ask God to show you a truth in the metaphor of sowing and reaping you may not have noticed up to this point. On your last reading, note words or phrases that stand out to you.

Read Psalm 126:4-6.

- What word or phrase stood out to you in this reading? If it is something that you have noted before, why do you think that phrase has stuck with you? If you noted it for the first time today, how does it inform your understanding of Psalm 126?

The psalmist describes a farmer and his fields. Despite the pain of the moment, God's children got up when the time came and sowed their seed into the ground with the hope of reaping a joyful harvest down the road. They needed to do this literally in order to eat once they arrived back in their decimated towns and villages after being exiled for seventy years. They needed to do it in other contexts as well.

I've always been struck by the phrase "carrying the bag of seed." The King James Version I grew up reading says they were "bearing precious seed." The implication is that the seeds were worth something. They were valuable.

- What is it about seeds, literally and figuratively, that makes them precious?

We will end our study this week by taking a deeper look at the metaphor of seed in Scripture. Our goal will be to identify the precious resources each of us has that we can sow—and that have been sown for us—for the future of God's kingdom.

When Genesis 1–2 tells us how God created the world, it specifies that God created not only plants, but seed-bearing plants. In other words, God created plants that create more plants. He would eventually create man and woman. They too were seed-bearing in that they would reproduce the next generation of their own kind.

Then God said, "Let the earth produce vegetation: seed-bearing plants and fruit trees on the earth bearing fruit with seed in it according to their kinds." And it was so. The earth produced vegetation: seed-bearing plants according to their kinds and trees bearing fruit with seed in it according to their kinds. And God saw that it was good. (Genesis 1:11-12)

- Why do you think God made plants to reproduce themselves when he created the Garden of Eden? Why not just create everything all at once as a closed system? This is a question I mull over a good bit myself. It's okay if you just think about it but don't have an answer.

Have you ever contemplated the miracle of a seed? Humanity has yet to harness life in any other way. We cannot recreate life in that which is dead. We cannot start new life in inanimate objects. But we can bring a new living thing into the world through seeds. The miracle of planting seeds to produce new life, be it plant, animal, or human, is the foundation of God's creation and his plan to sustain it. God created plants and people that would bring forth offspring that would produce the next season (or generation) of plants and people, declaring it all very good. Planting seeds today still reflects God's good design for the world, despite humanity's fall.

- What insight does the sowing and reaping metaphor in Psalm 126:4-6 give you for your current season of life?

- Your fields to work may be far removed from rural farmland, and your seeds to sow may not come in seed packets or result in green plants. But God's instructions to Adam and Eve still apply to us today. He told them to work and protect their fields, to cultivate and multiply (Genesis

1:28; 2:15). Do you see the potential when in joint venture with God, you take the tiny, precious resource of seed he has provided and plant with an eye to the harvest? The work may be hard, but that does not make it bad. In fact, you and I were created for this very thing. What precious seed do you see around you? What fields can you cultivate and tend despite your continued grief?

- Why are we tempted to stop sowing seeds and tending our figurative fields during seasons of weeping and lament? What keeps you from sowing seeds in your current realms of influence?

As we close today, ask God to open your eyes to the "precious seed" in your life. Ask him to remove the internal and external barriers that keep you from putting your hand to the plow. Ask him to help you invest the resources you've been given, even amid your grief and lament.

GENESIS 41:46-52 — DAY 4

TODAY, LET'S LOOK at another person in the Bible who, in terms of the language of Psalm 126, sowed seeds even as he wept. Joseph's story is told in Genesis 37–50. He was the favored son of his father Jacob, betrayed by his jealous brothers, and sold into slavery in Egypt. Unjustly accused of attempted rape, he sat forgotten in a foul prison for years. Then, he had a stunning reversal of fortune when the Egyptian king made Joseph second-in-command in the kingdom. But Joseph still felt deep grief over his losses, even after his rise to power.

That's the context for the passage we will read today from Genesis 41. Read it three times slowly. Between each reading, ask God to open your eyes to the ways Joseph's experience sheds light on the value of continuing to work for the kingdom through ongoing suffering and grief. On your last reading, note words or phrases that stand out to you.

Read Genesis 41:46-52.

- What words or phrases stood out to you in this reading?

Given our study of Psalm 126, you may be able to guess the portion of this text on which we will focus. Joseph named his second son Ephraim. His name is from the Hebrew for "double fruitfulness." Joseph was doubly fruitful in having two sons. But he was also fruitful as he gathered harvest for the people to feed them through the coming famine.

But where was Joseph fruitful? In the land of his affliction—the land of his misery, the land of his oppression (v. 52). When Joseph named his son, he was still captive in Egypt, separated from his father and little brother. He was still not in control of his own future. Joseph was fruitful though he was not done suffering. He was fruitful in the midst of his suffering.

- In what ways can you identify with the language "in the land of my affliction"? What is the land of your affliction?

- When I first read this passage, I didn't like the name Ephraim. I didn't want to be fruitful in the land of my affliction. I wanted to be fruitful in a better land, the land I desired for myself. I wanted to be free of my affliction, not fruitful in the midst of it. How do you react to the phrase "fruitful in the land of my affliction"?

- Yesterday, we discussed the hurdles to flourishing we face amid our own suffering. They can feel like barriers to any type of good work for God's kingdom. What barriers to sowing seed and harvesting fruit, figuratively and literally, do you think Joseph faced during his life in Egypt?

Despite our desire to be released from the circumstances that afflict us, there must come a point in our suffering and grief when we acknowledge what God has allowed in our life and submit to him. It benefits our souls to recognize that, like it or not, the land of our affliction is the land God has given us to sow. The beauty of Joseph's story is that meaningful work and harvest were still possible amid horribly broken circumstances. The name Ephraim is full of hope.

- Joseph didn't outline exactly how God helped him, yet God was the one Joseph named who made him fruitful despite his harsh circumstances. Remember that though your circumstances are different than Joseph's, your God is the same. How was God the agent in Joseph's fruitfulness? If you are unfamiliar with his story, read Genesis 39:1-6 and Genesis 41.

As we close today, repeat the prayer we closed with yesterday on day three. Ask God to open your eyes to the precious seed in your life that he would have you to sow. Ask him to open your eyes to the ways you can be, or maybe already are, fruitful despite the hard land you live in right now. Ask him what it looks like for you to sow in tears. Ask him to make you fruitful despite all the ways you groan under the weight of all that is wrong in the world.

We have reached the last day of our eight week study on psalms of lament. Would you take a moment now to stop and ponder how your thoughts about lament have changed over the weeks of this study? What have you learned that has been helpful as you process your own suffering?

We defined suffering as our groaning under the weight of all that is wrong in the world, and in our lives in particular, since the fall of humanity. We groan at times with grief too deep for words. We have learned from seven psalms of lament and one psalm of ascent—preserved over time by God—that we do not groan alone. These psalms give us words to speak to God when we feel unable to put words to the grief we feel. The invitation from God is to come to him boldly in our time of need to find the grace and mercy we desperately need (Hebrews 4:16).

This week's psalm, Psalm 126, is a helpful final psalm for us, because it moves us toward functioning again. However, this psalm doesn't describe the movement toward functioning as if our grief has finished. The psalmist hasn't closed the door on his lament and started over with a new outlook. Instead, he paints a realistic picture of a future that includes long-term grief and lament. This text speaks to the reality that there are some losses we will not stop mourning until we sit in the shade of the tree of life as God himself wipes the tears from our eyes (Revelation 22).

The "seed" metaphor we find in Psalm 126 and throughout Scripture is an apt description of the gifts we sow amid our grief. But we will end our study today not by looking at seeds for us to sow. Instead, we will look at the Seed that was sown for us. In speaking of himself, Jesus told his disciples,

> The hour has come for the Son of Man to be glorified. Truly I tell you, unless a grain of wheat falls to the ground and dies, it remains by itself. But if it dies, it produces much fruit. (John 12:23-24)

Today, we will read a longer passage. Read it three times slowly. Ask God to help you see how Jesus' death, burial, and resurrection equips you, in the words of Joseph, to be fruitful in the land of your affliction. Mark words or phrases that stand out to you.

Read 1 Corinthians 15:20-22, 35-45.

- What words or phrases did you note? Why did that language stand out to you?

In the verses that come just before this passage in 1 Corinthians 15, Paul wrote about how Christ's resurrection is a necessity for our salvation. Paul insisted that if Jesus died in our place and went into the ground, staying there dead, our faith is worthless (v. 17), and we should be pitied (v. 19). This makes sense when we remember that the first mention of Christ in Genesis 3:15 called him the Seed. I can tell you from much experience around farmers that there is nothing sadder than seeds planted in the ground that never burst forth. Every bit of effort is wasted if the seed doesn't germinate.

Jesus died and was planted in the grave, but he also germinated. He came back to life, and he produces much fruit!

- Paul called Jesus the firstfruits of the resurrection (1 Corinthians 15:20). What is the significance of this description?

- If Jesus was resurrected from the dead, and his resurrection is the firstfruits, what does that mean for you as you face your own ongoing grief over the losses in your life?

The question for those early New Testament Christians in Corinth was what would happen to them when they died. What was the hope of the gospel of Jesus Christ if it didn't free the Corinthians from their problems right away? What was the hope of this good news if they and their loved ones still got sick, still experienced oppression, and still died? Paul was adamant that this church understand the necessity of both the death and resurrection of Jesus. Though these Christians would continue to suffer, there was hope beyond the grave. And because Christ is the firstfruits, we too will experience resurrection.

We too will be raised, and we will be raised in much better form than we were put into the ground.

> Sown in corruption, raised in incorruption; sown in dishonor, raised in glory; sown in weakness, raised in power; sown a natural body, raised a spiritual body. (1 Corinthians 15:42-44)

- How do these verses speak to the losses you currently experience? What hope do they give you for the future?

Paul insists that the resurrection gives us great hope. Our hope is that the corpse of our believing loved one (as well as our own) isn't simply a corpse; it is a seed. And because Christ burst forth from the grave, it will too.

The Sower and his Seed are the great allegory for both life and death, for living and dying. Despite our current griefs, we sow the seed God has given us, and we tend the ground to protect the harvest. This is the great, meaningful work of our lives here on earth. When we come to the end of our lives, we are sown too, with the promise that we will germinate with perfect bodies just as Christ did.

In the meantime, suffering friend, get up, plant your seeds despite your tears, and tend your land as you wait for the harvest. Cultivate faithfulness in the land God has given you. As Jesus germinated and sprouted from the grave, so will you.

Those who sow in tears will reap with shouts of joy. (Psalm 126:5)

Let's close our study in a final prayer. Personalize it to make it your own.

Father, I am still mourning. I still feel deep grief from which I long to be freed. I feel the heavy weights on myself, my loved ones, and my community from all that broke at the fall of humanity, and I groan. Thank you for the laments in Scripture that have guided me to bring my groaning directly to you. Thank you for your supernatural grace that helps me persevere.

One day, I will sit in the shade of the tree of life as you gently wipe the tears from my face. Until then, help me keep sowing the seeds you have given me. Jesus is the seed sown for us, and because he came alive out of the ground, I have hope that the seeds that seem dead or dormant in my own life will too. Show me what you would have me to do in this season. Help me put my hand to the plow in the fields of your kingdom.

By your supernatural grace, I believe I will reap in joy.

CLOSING BENEDICTION

Now to him who is able to do above and beyond all that we ask or think according to the power that works in us—to him be glory in the church and in Christ Jesus to all generations, forever and ever. Amen. (Ephesians 3:20-21)

FIGURE CREDITS

Week 1: Fabulous watercolor landscape: Pobytov/DigitalVision Vectors via Getty Images

Week 2: Aerial roots in painted canvas: Zu Sanchez Photography/Moment via Getty Images

Week 3: A pathway: Zu Sanchez Photography/Moment via Getty Images

Week 4: Oil painted winter forest: Pobytov/Digital Vision Vectors via Getty Images

Week 5: Watercolor autumn landscape: Pobytoc/Digital Vision Vectors via Getty Images

Week 6: Autumn morning in the forest, acrylic painting: Pobytov/DigitalVision Vectors via Getty Images

Week 7: Summer sunset, watercolor painting: Pobytov/DigitalVision Vectors via Getty Images

Week 8: The great tree—stock illustration: Pobytov/DigitalVision Vectors via Getty Images

Mountains landscape, the Negev Desert, Israel, photo by Avi Theret on Unsplash

TRANSFORM YOUR BIBLE STUDY EXPERIENCE

Did you enjoy this Bible study? Here's some good news: there are even more IVP Bible Study Experience volumes to help you and your small group uncover the depths of God's Word in a whole new light.

SCAN HERE for IVP Bible Studies information and special discounts!

These studies are designed to take you deeper into God's Word, inviting you to discern how to apply the content to your daily life. Each one is formatted as a beautiful workbook with plenty of white space for individual reflection as well as inspiring full-color images and graphic elements. Continue your in-depth study of Scripture with an IVP Bible Study Experience volume!

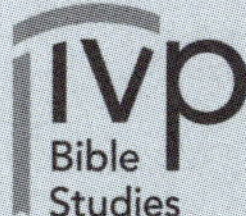